The Black E Governmental Learning

The Learning Spiral— A Concept to Organize Learning in Governments

by

Raoul Blindenbacher

in collaboration with Bidjan Nashat

http://www.worldbank.org/ieg/learningspiral

Copyright © 2010 The International Bank for Reconstruction and Development/The World Bank
1818 H Street, N.W.
Washington, D.C. 20433
Telephone: 202-473-1000
Internet: www.worldbank.org
E-mail: feedback@worldbank.org

All rights reserved

1 2 3 4 13 12 11 10

This volume is a product of the authors. The findings, interpretations, and conclusions expressed in this volume do not necessarily reflect the views of the Executive Directors of The World Bank or the governments they represent. This volume does not support any general inferences beyond the scope of the text, including any inferences about the World Bank Group's past, current, or prospective overall performance.

The World Bank Group does not guarantee the accuracy of the data included in this work. The boundaries, colors, denominations, and other information shown on any map in this work do not imply any judgement on the part of The World Bank concerning the legal status of any territory or the endorsement or acceptance of such boundaries.

Rights and Permissions

The material in this publication is copyrighted. Copying and/or transmitting portions or all of this work without permission may be a violation of applicable law. The International Bank for Reconstruction and Development / The World Bank encourages dissemination of its work and will normally grant permission to reproduce portions of the work promptly.

For permission to photocopy or reprint any part of this work, please send a request with complete information to the Copyright Clearance Center Inc., 222 Rosewood Drive, Danvers, MA 01923, USA; telephone: 978-750-8400; fax: 978-750-4470; Internet: www.copyright.com.

All other queries on rights and licenses, including subsidiary rights, should be addressed to the Office of the Publisher, The World Bank, 1818 H Street NW, Washington, DC 20433, USA; fax: 202-522-2422; e-mail: pubrights@worldbank.org.

Cover: The book cover has been generated with Wordle (http://www.wordle.net), an online tool for generating "word clouds" from text. Word clouds give greater prominence to words that appear more frequently in the source text. The entire text of this book was used to generate the cover word cloud. The images created by the Wordle application are licensed under a Creative Commons Attribution license.

ISBN-13: 978-0-8213-8453-4
e-ISBN: 978-0-8213-8474-9
DOI: 10.1596/978-0-8213-8453-4

Library of Congress Cataloging-in-Publication Data

Blindenbacher, Raoul.
 The black box of governmental learning : the learning spiral—a concept to organize learning in governments / by Raoul Blindenbacher in collaboration with Bidjan Nashat.
   p. cm.
 Includes bibliographical references.
 ISBN 978-0-8213-8453-4 — ISBN 978-0-8213-8474-9 (electronic)
 1. Public administration—Evaluation. 2. Organizational learning. 3. Action learning. 4. Government executives—In-service training. I. Nashat, Bidjan, 1979- II. World Bank. III. Title.
 JF1525.O74B55 2010
 352.6'69dc22
                                   2010019105

World Bank InfoShop
E-mail: pic@worldbank.org
Telephone: 202-458-5454
Facsimile: 202-522-1500

Independent Evaluation Group
Communication, Strategy, and Learning
E-mail: ieg@worldbank.org
Telephone: 202-458-4497
Facsimile: 202-522-3125

Printed on Recycled Paper

The Black Box of Governmental Learning Outline

Foreword

Preface

Executive Summary

Chapter 1   Introduction

Part I—Analytical and Theoretical Considerations

Chapter 2   Analytical Concepts of Governmental Learning

Chapter 3   Theoretical Concepts of Governmental Learning

Chapter 4   A New Concept of Governmental Learning—The Learning Spiral

Part II—Practical Application

Chapter 5   International Conference

Chapter 6   Multiyear Global Program Roundtables

Chapter 7   Study Tour

Chapter 8   Evaluation-Based Workshop

Chapter 9   Multimedia Training and E-Learning Initiative

Chapter 10   Conclusions and Outlook

Table of Contents

Foreword xi

Preface xiii

Executive Summary xvii

1 Introduction 1
   1.1 Why Learning in Governments? 1
   1.2 A Concept to Organize Learning in Governments 3
   1.3 Outline of the Book 5

Part I   Analytical and Theoretical Considerations 9

2 Analytical Concepts of Governmental Learning 11
   2.1 Historical Analysis 11
       2.1.1 Origins 12
       2.1.2 Learning Approaches 16
   2.2 Today's Practices 19
       2.2.1 Learning Approaches Today 20
       2.2.2 Practical Application 24
       2.2.3 Types of Events 29
   2.3 Particularities and Lessons 34
       2.3.1 Particularities and Barriers 34
       2.3.2 Lessons from Past and Current Practices.. 39

3 Theoretical Concepts of Governmental Learning 43
   3.1 Democratic Government, Democratic Governance, and Governmental Learning 43

        3.1.1   Concepts of Democratic Government and Democratic Governance 44
        3.1.2   Policy Analysis and Governmental Learning. 47
   3.2   Knowledge in Democratic Governance............. 49
        3.2.1   Concepts of Knowledge Creation 50
        3.2.2   Knowledge Creation in Democratic Governance............................. 53
   3.3   Learning Theories............................... 57
        3.3.1   Individual Learning 58
        3.3.2   Organizational Learning 62

4 A New Concept of Governmental Learning—The Learning Spiral 67

   4.1   Learning System and Learning Process 67
        4.1.1   Learning System. 68
        4.1.2   The Learning Process and Its Methodology .. 69
   4.2   Stages of the Learning Spiral 73
        Stage 1: Conceptualization 73
        Stage 2: Triangulation 74
        Stage 3: Accommodation 76
        Stage 4: Internalization 77
        Stage 5: Externalization 78
        Stage 6: Reconceptualization 80
        Stage 7: Transformation 81
        Stage 8: Configuration 82
   4.3   Practice of the Learning Spiral.................... 84
        4.3.1   Template and Organization 84
        4.3.2   Evaluation and Results Framework.......... 88

Part II Practical Application 93

5 International Conference 95

   5.1   Conference Reader—Conceptualization Stage 95
   5.2   Sixty Federal and Decentralized Countries—Triangulation Stage 97

5.3	Introduction of the Conference Reader—Accommodation Stage	98
5.4	Work Sessions—Internalization Stage	99
5.5	Dialogue Tables—Externalization Stage	101
5.6	Expert Summaries—Reconceptualization Stage	104
5.7	Interactive Plenary Panels—Transformation Stage	104
5.8	Conference Proceedings—Configuration Stage	105
5.9	Final Comments and Evaluation	105
Box 1:	Reflections from Robert D. Ebel, Deputy Chief Financial Officer and Chief Economist of the Washington, DC, Government	107
Box 2:	Reflections from Bob Rae, Former Premier of Ontario and Current Member of the Parliament of Canada	109

6 Multiyear Global Program Roundtables ... 111

6.1	Theme Template—Conceptualization Stage	112
6.2	Twelve Federal Countries—Triangulation Stage	113
6.3	Program Manual—Accommodation Stage	113
6.4	Country Roundtables—Internalization Stage	114
6.5	International Roundtable—Externalization Stage	114
6.6	Theme Paper—Reconceptualization Stage	116
6.7	Online Discussion Forum—Transformation Stage	117
6.8	Handbook and Booklet Series—Configuration Stage	117
6.9	Final Comments and Evaluation	118
Box 3:	Reflections from Arnold Koller, Former President of Switzerland	119

7 Study Tour ... 123

7.1	2005 Iraqi Constitution—Conceptualization Stage	123
7.2	Four Judiciary Systems—Triangulation Stage	124
7.3	Study Tour Program—Accommodation Stage	125

7.4 Field Trips—Internalization Stage 126
7.5 Reflection Sessions—Externalization Stage 127
7.6 Vision of Iraqi Judiciary System—
     Reconceptualization Stage 127
7.7 Political Roadmap—Transformation Stage 128
7.8 CD-ROM—Configuration Stage 128
7.9 Final Comments and Evaluation 129
Box 4: Reflections from Medhat Al Mahmoud, Chief
     Justice of the Federal Supreme Court and
     President of the Higher Judicial Council of Iraq . . . 130

8 Evaluation-Based Workshop 133

8.1 Four Evaluation Reports—Conceptualization
     Stage 134
8.2 Eight African Countries—Triangulation Stage . . . 135
8.3 Concept Note and Guidance Note—
     Accommodation Stage 135
8.4 Plenary Sessions—Internalization Stage 137
8.5 Breakout Groups—Externalization Stage 138
8.6 Review of Evaluation Reports—
     Reconceptualization Stage 139
8.7 Action Plan—Transformation Stage 139
8.8 Brochure—Configuration Stage 139
8.9 Final Comments and Evaluation 140
Box 5: Reflections from Ato Ahmed Mohammed Ali,
     Director of Planning and Programming
     Directorate, Ministry of Capacity Building of
     the Government of Ethiopia 141

9 Multimedia Training and E-Learning Initiative 145

9.1 Core Learning Components—Conceptualization
     Stage 146
9.2 Global Target Audience—Triangulation Stage 147
9.3 Users' Manual—Accommodation Stage 148
9.4 Online Questionnaire—Internalization Stage 149
9.5 Online Dialogue Exchange—Externalization 150
9.6 Process Monitoring—Reconceptualization Stage . 152

9.7	Scenario Exercises and Rapid Results Approach—Transformation Stage	152
9.8	Revision of CLCs—Configuration Stage	154
9.9	Final Comments and Evaluation	154
Box 6:	Reflections from Govindan G. Nair, Lead Economist, Public–Private Partnerships, World Bank Institute	155

10 Conclusions and Outlook 157

10.1	Conclusions	157
10.2	Outlook	159

Bibliography 163

List of Boxes, Figures, Tables, and Pictures 179

Author Biographies 183

Foreword

Ten years ago, world leaders agreed on an ambitions set of development goals to be reached by 2015. Although progress has been made, the Millennium Development Goals remain elusive for many countries and their citizens. If more rapid progress is to be made in the future, learning from success and failure will be crucial for governments, international organizations, and civil society organizations as they try to improve the livelihoods of their citizens around the world.

By making learning and accountability its two main purposes, evaluation tries to make a contribution to this process. Whereas accountability directs our attention backward, learning requires us to focus on how to improve results in the future. Evaluators have developed an excellent range of rigorous tools and methods to find out what has worked and what has not, and we spend much of our time and resources on the process of gathering evidence and producing knowledge. However, we are far less certain that we have all the tools and methods to help organizations and stakeholders learn from evaluations to improve development results.

The Learning Spiral has been developed to help fill the gap between the creation of knowledge and its application by concerned stakeholders. It combines theoretical approaches with individual, organizational, and governmental learning. It has a sound foundation from both a theoretical and an empirical perspective. The Learning Spiral is grounded in theories that have been developed and tested successfully. At its center is the recognition that learning is a nonlinear and highly contextual process. It requires no less effort to learn from evaluations and to apply knowledge to improve future outcomes than it does to conduct evaluations in the first place.

At the World Bank Group's Independent Evaluation Group, we have further developed and applied the Learning Spiral over the past two years as a tool for learning from evaluations together with our stakeholders all over the world. This book enriches the theoretical basis for the Learning Spiral with practical experience in bringing about change based on evaluation findings.

We have worked with clients to develop structured learning events that have taken us to Nigeria, where we focused on state-level engagement in federal states, as well as to Washington, DC, and Addis Ababa, where stakeholders from 10 African countries exchanged challenges and solutions on public sector reform. As a result of applying the Learning Spiral, we have been able to step further in the direction of complementing our mandate for accountability with learning. Focusing just on the former is like standing on one leg—both, accountability and learning, are needed to run. We believe that evaluations can make a considerable difference in helping our stakeholders understand what works and what does not and it is for that reason that we have started dialogues on how to improve development results through evaluation.

Hans-Martin Boehmer
Manager, Communication, Learning, and Strategy
World Bank Independent Evaluation Group

Preface

The Black Box of Governmental Learning is an attempt to close the gap between practice and the theory of how to organize learning events for governments in the 21st century. It is the result of my personal experiences over a decade of organizing conferences, e-learning events, study tours, training, etc. for all levels of government, in numerous countries around the world, and on all sorts of themes related to democratic governance.

In many ways *The Black Box of Governmental Learning* represents a research project in itself: In the first part of the book, all major analytical and theoretical considerations related to the topic are enumerated; I subsequently review them in a qualitative content analysis. Based on this examination, I have developed the Learning Spiral as it presents today, a heuristic concept that provides a template to organize governmental learning events. In the second part of the book, the practical relevance of this concept is verified through descriptions of its application in five selected learning activities.

The Black Box of Governmental Learning could not have been written without the thousands of participants who agreed to engage and share their personal experiences in such learning events. They were eager to learn from each other to improve their knowledge of democratic governance and by doing so to better serve their constituents. They all deserve my deepest respect and gratitude. I hope they will continue participating in such learning processes and encourage others to follow their example. I also hope they stay actively engaged in the many networks that were created in the aftermath of these activities.

The fact that I had the opportunity to organize learning activities in the first place is only possible thanks to the vision of a few individuals who risked organizing high-level governmental learning events differently than had been done in the past. Among these individuals, I would like to point out Peter Habluezel, the former head of the Swiss Federal Department of Human Resources, who allowed me to organize the first event for the top management of the Swiss federal civil service administration. The first application of the Learning Spiral on a truly international level with high-ranking participants occurred at the 2002 International Conference on Federalism and was only feasible because of the strong support of Arnold Koller, former President of Switzerland, as well as other leading Swiss representatives, such as Canisius Braun, Walter Fust, and, in particular, Luzius Mader.

On an institutional level these initiatives were backed up by the Swiss Federal Department of Foreign Affairs and the Department of Justice and later on by international organizations such as the Forum of Federations, the World Bank's Independent Evaluation Group (IEG), and the World Bank Institute. In particular, I recognize IEG's Director-General Vinod Thomas, Senior Manager Ali Khadr, and managers Klaus Tilmes and his very engaged successor Hans-Martin Boehmer; they were all a tremendous support. They not only allowed me to apply the Learning Spiral in evaluation-based learning events, but also facilitated the publication of the concept and by doing so have made it available to a wider audience.

The success of such learning events depends to a high degree on a multitude of individuals who lead and/or contribute to their realization. The following list of people (in alphabetical order) represents just a small number of the many colleagues who played an outstanding role in the organization of these activities. Inside the World Bank, I would like to mention Konstantin Atanesyan, Mel Blunt, Gita Gopal, Moira Hart-Poliquin, Svetlana Markova, Cia Sjetnan, and Anwar Shah. From outside the Bank I thank Barbara Brook, Rupak Chattopadhyay, Abigail Ostien, Chandra Pasma, and Cheryl Sanders (all from the Forum of Federations), Franz Hierlemann, Jakob Huber, Andrea Iff, and Amitabha Pande.

Needless to say, the organization of learning events stands and falls with administrative support. Among the many quiet helpers in the background I would like to point out in the World Bank Princess Moore-Lewis, Maria Padrino, and Esperanza Sadiua, as well as Rhonda Dumas and Nicole Pedersen from the Forum of Federations.

As the book is based on theoretical and practical reflections, I depended on a great number of colleagues who represent different fields in academia as well as practice, many of them covering both spheres. Among these individuals who offered advice on how to develop and describe the concept in the book are, from the World Bank, Andreas Foerster, Guenter Meinert, Jan Rielaender, Bahar Salimova, Janardan Prasad Singh; I also recognize academics like Matthew Andrews (Harvard University), Reinhart Fatke (University of Zuerich), Thomas

Fleiner (University of Fribourg), Nico Steytler (University of the Western Cape), and Ron Watts (Queens University).

The personal testimonies given by selected individuals who actively participated in the different learning events described are of great value to the book. The authors who summarize their experiences and lessons learned are Robert D. Ebel, Arnold Koller, Medhat Al Mahmoud, Govindan Nair, Ato Ahmed Mohammed Ali, and Bob Rae. The significance of these testimonials is particularly important because they were written one or more years after each event took place; the authors have therefore been able to reflect on the long-term impact of the knowledge learned.

The content is the backbone of a book. However, the way knowledge is transformed into words and phrases can make the difference if a book is readable or not. I am therefore deeply grateful to the IEG editor Heather Dittbrenner, who reviewed *The Black Box of Governmental Learning* regarding its style and language.

Writing a book has always its price, which often tends to be quietly paid by a family that stands behind an author. It is therefore very much in my heart to thank my wife Franziska for her continuous motivation to my finishing that book, even though I sometimes felt I could not do so. Let me also mention my son Olivier and daughter Sophie, who often made me laugh and sometimes frown too, when I thought I needed quiet time and did not realize that I had to stop working to clear my head with the really important things that life offers.

And last I would like to point out my friend and colleague Bidjan Nashat, who greatly contributed to *The Black Box of Governmental Learning*. He was always there when I needed him to share and develop new ideas. With his open-minded and unconventional thinking he helped me overcome many obstacles and challenges. He also made an exceptional contribution by writing the section of the book about Evaluation and Results Framework. With Bidjan I found a unique kinship; he shares my unshakable belief that governmental learning events can contribute to the performance of democratic governance and by doing so help reduce poverty and enhance sustainable development in governments.

Raoul Blindenbacher
Washington, DC

Executive Summary

There are more poor people and poverty reaches further into middle-income countries around the world than ever before. Adequate governmental capacity development is considered one of the critical missing factors in current efforts to reduce poverty and, by doing so, to meet the Millennium Development Goals. If the development of sustainable capacity is not given greater attention in the near future, development efforts in the poorest countries are expected to fail even if they are supported with substantially increased funding.

One effective way to improve the quality of democratic governments is by their learning from the past and from each other's experiences. But to what extent are governments capable of and/or willing to learn? And if they are, what are they supposed to learn—and how? Is the way they learn different from the way individuals or organizations learn? Under what conditions do they learn best, and to what extent can learning events enhance their capacities to improve the performance of their public sectors? These and many related questions are examined in *The Black Box of Governmental Learning*.

Facing poverty and ever-increasing local and global problems such as financial crises, climate change, and pandemics, democratic governments worldwide must find better ways to provide public goods and services to their citizens—and thus reduce poverty, accelerate economic growth, and improve sustainable development. There is a widely shared conviction among practitioners and scholars alike that governments in both developed and developing countries do have the capacity and are willing to learn from their pasts and/or from other countries' experiences. One means of doing this is in formal pre-arranged learning events like conferences, e-learning, study tours, roundtables, training, and workshops, which are an affordable and promising way to make governments more effective.

However, little is known about how governments learn best or what exactly makes them change their behavior in a deliberate and targeted way. Governments consist of thousands of state officials and numerous institutional units—the executive branch, parliaments, the judiciary, and the civil service—which function under unique political conditions and environments. Experience has shown that they learn differently than individuals and/or organizations do. Governmental learning goes beyond individual and organizational learning approaches and is considered a complex and hard-to-conceptualize matter; it must address many cultural, economical, political, religious, and social particularities, psychological barriers, and practical constraints that might hinder or even prevent learning at all.

The Black Box of Governmental Learning introduces the Learning Spiral, a new concept for organizing efficient prearranged learning events for governments. The Learning Spiral—a heuristic and multidisciplinary concept—has been developed over the past decade for national and international governmental learning events. It was created through an ongoing dialectical process, where an original theory-based concept was applied in practice, reviewed, and subsequently reapplied in a forthcoming event. This process was repeated on an ongoing basis in numerous events held in developed and developing countries all over the world, with thousands of participants from all levels of governments and nongovernmental organizations.

The Learning Spiral was conceptualized in a template consisting of eight consecutive stages: Conceptualization, Triangulation, Accommodation, Internalization, Externalization, Reconceptualization, Transformation, and Configuration. When these stages are performed, a didactical process is established that encourages behavioral change in governmental institutions, their members, and representatives from involved nongovernmental organizations and interest groups. The template serves as a practical guideline to organize governmental learning events. It offers general directions on designing a learning process and should therefore be applicable to any form and type of governmental learning activity.

The didactic concept of the Learning Spiral is based on an analysis of past and current experiences of how governments learn, the particular knowledge they learn, and how knowledge gets created and transferred to the learning actors. It further takes into account contemporary theories of political history, policy analysis, pedagogy, and sociology, as well as individual, organizational, and governmental learning concepts.

The practical application of the eight stages involves an elaborate process that includes the planning and designing of a particular learning event. The design is based on an analysis of the knowledge to be learned, usually state-of-the-art or evaluation-based knowledge regarding the issue at hand. The design also takes into account the political environment where the event is taking place, and it requires a deliberate selection of the individual learning actors and the governmental and nongovernmental institutions involved. This approach requires close attention to the interrelationship between the knowledge content of a learning event and the design of its process.

A major characteristic of this type of learning event is its facilitation by a learning broker who oversees all aspects of the event organization. This includes the logistics, the content preparation, the drafting and carrying through of the agenda, the moderation of the learning sessions, and the follow-up activities. Another important feature of the Learning Spiral is that there are no designated speakers. The distinction between knowledge holders and knowledge recipients becomes dispensable. Every participant is considered an active contributor who, whenever it appears appropriate, shares his or her experiences. With this kind of structure, every participant gets unlimited access to the collective wealth of the shared knowledge.

The effects of the applied Learning Spiral are threefold: The primary effect is that governments' access to the latest knowledge in democratic governance is enhanced and can be applied in concrete, practical action. A second effect is that—because of the iterative character of the learning process—the knowledge to be learned is always validated and updated in real time to include the latest existing experiences on the subject. And a third effect is that participation in the learning process evokes a sense of social belonging among the learning actors, which often leads to the creation of social networks, where governments continue to share their latest experiences and by doing so launch the next spin of the Learning Spiral.

To make the concept of the Learning Spiral accessible for practical use, *The Black Box of Governmental Learning* presents a number of case studies that show how the Learning Spiral has been successfully applied. The examples range from an international conference with several hundred participants, among them numerous heads of state and government, to a small evaluation-based workshop for African policy makers from 10 different countries, to a multimedia training and e-learning initiative. Each case study is supplemented by a first-hand account from a high-level participant, such as a former president, a member of parliament, or a Supreme Court chief justice.

The Black Box of Governmental Learning is directed toward practitioners in governments, such as members of cabinets, parliaments, and courts; civil servants and politicians; civil society and private sector organizations; and international organizations. It provides a theory-guided and practice-approved comprehensive template for how to organize effective learning events for governments in the 21st century.

The concept of the Learning Spiral is a work in progress, and it has to be adapted to changes and new findings in practice and research in governmental learning. The Learning Spiral can be adapted to specific settings and government situations; it will evolve during use depending on changes and new findings in practice and research, and as governments continue to learn, it will adapt itself to those new situations. Practitioners and theoreticians are therefore invited to engage in the dialogue launched herein to further improve the learning capacities of governments, and by doing so, illuminate the black box of governmental learning.

1 Introduction

The Black Box of Governmental Learning is the result of an intense and creative dialogue with colleagues in and outside the World Bank about the need for and purpose of governments to learn and how such learning can be made more effective. There was broad consensus that much more reflection is required in particular about the settings in which organized learning in governments is taking place. The Learning Spiral, presented and explained in this book, is a concept that provides a comprehensive procedure to organize learning events specifically designed for democratic governments. The concept is a theory-based and practice-approved contribution that can open the black box of complex and elusive transactions and processes that characterize governmental learning.

1.1 Why Learning in Governments?

The World Bank's development indicators conclude that today there are more poor people living on this planet than ever (World Bank 2008). It seems that despite all efforts by the international community, the United Nation's Millennium Development Goals (MDGs), which aim to reduce poverty and increase sustainable economic growth, will not be achieved by 2015 (UN 2000a, 2000b).[1] Among the many vital factors that do have critical impact in reducing poverty is the quality of the public sector (IEG 2008a, 2008b). There is no doubt that when governments perform poorly, the consequences are wasted resources; undelivered services; and denial of social, legal, and economic protection for citizens, especially the poor. Poor governance, meanwhile, is seen as the single most important factor in eradicating poverty and promoting development (Grindle 2004). *Democratic governance* is understood as the term that sum-

---

1. In 1998, the General Assembly of the United Nations (UN) decided to convene the Millennium Summit as an integral part of the Millennium Assembly of the United Nations. In that summit, held on September 6, 2000, the developing countries, donor nations, and the international financial institutions agreed to the MDGs, which aim to halve extreme poverty from 1990 levels by 2015 (UN 2000a).

marizes all managerial responsibilities of a government in delivering public services and goods that contribute to the safety and well-being of citizens under a given set of democratic principles and rules.[2]

Supporting governments as they seek to improve the performance of their democratic governmental system has become a priority in donor and development policies and is seen as the most promising factor of intervention.[3] The international community concludes that if the development of sustainable capacity in governments is not given greater and more careful attention in the near future, development efforts in many of the poorest countries will fail even if funding is substantially increased over time (DAC 2006). Thus, governments all over the world, with the support of national and multilateral development and donor organizations, have to strive for better and more efficient ways to improve their performance in democratic governance. This includes in particular the implementation of a broad range of democratic principles, the delivery of adequate services and goods, and the management of appropriate governmental institutions.

One effective means of improving the quality of democratic governance is by learning from past practices and/or from other governments' experiences (IEG 2008a, 2008d). Such concerted learning helps governments avoid repeating mistakes and encourages them to adopt successful practices from others. Learning in these terms means behavioral change—in an intended direction—by a government on the level of its policy actors as well as its respective institutional bodies. But to what extent are governments capable of and/or willing to learn? And if they can/are, what do they want to learn—and how? Is the way they learn different from the way individuals or organizations learn? Under what conditions do they learn best, and to what extent can learning events for

---

2. The term *democratic governance* has been extensively discussed in the theoretical literature (March and Olsen 1995; Cohen and Rogers 1992; Dreze and Sen 1989). However, the understanding here is based on practice-oriented definitions given by the major national and international donor and development organizations (SIDA 2003; World Bank 1998; UNDP 1994; Punyaratabandhy 2004). For further elaborations of the term, see subsections 2.1.1, 3.1.1, and 3.2.2.
3. See, for example, the 2005 Paris Declaration on Aid Effectiveness, which was organized under the auspices of the Development Assistance Committee (DAC) of the Organisation for Economic Co-operation and Development (OECD) as well as the 2008 Accra Agenda for Action.

governments enhance their capacities to improve their performance in democratic governance? And last, what are governments? Are they the sum of their members' respective policy actors, or the sum of their institutional bodies, or both together (Kemp and Weehuizen 2005)?

These and many related questions are examined in *The Black Box of Governmental Learning*. This book is based on the belief that governments are willing to and convinced of the need to improve their capacities by learning in democratic governance.[4] As discussed later, this position is based on historical, theoretical and empirical evidence. However, governmental learning does not just happen naturally (Rist 1994). It must be planned and carried through in a deliberate, targeted, and theory-based manner to have real impact on performance (IEG 2008a). Also, governmental learning can take place in many ways. One important mode is formal and prearranged activities, such as conferences, roundtables, study tours, training, workshops, and—increasingly—e-learning activities.

1.2   A Concept to Organize Learning in Governments

To date, little is known about the complex combinations between who in a government has to learn what knowledge in which kind of didactical procedures (Kemp and Weehuizen 2005). Often referred to as a black box, learning in governments is considered hard to operationalize and conceptualize. An effective learning concept must address all individual and institutional aspects of a governmental system, which are related to the given knowledge to be learned. Such a system includes the executive branch, the civil service, political parties, formal oversight institutions such as parliaments and the judiciary, as well as a broad range of civil society and private sector organizations like the media, business associations, and so forth.

All these governmental and nongovernmental bodies function under unique political conditions and environments. A comprehensive concept of governmental learning must therefore also consider cultural, political, religious, and social particularities, as well as psychological barriers

---

4. Other authors who support this thesis are, for example, Kemp and Weehuizen (2005), Cowan et al. (2000), and Rist (1994).

and practical constraints that might hinder or even prevent learning at all. The Learning Spiral presented in this book is a practical concept that is designed to take up many of these issues by offering a template that, when applied, allows the organization of effective governmental learning events.

The Learning Spiral—a heuristic and multidisciplinary concept—has been developed for national and international governmental learning activities over the past decade. It was created through an ongoing dialectical process, where an original theory-based concept was applied in practice, reviewed, and reapplied in a subsequent event. This process was repeated in numerous events held in developed and developing countries all over the world, with thousands of participants from all levels of government and nongovernmental organizations.

The Learning Spiral template consists of eight consecutive stages: Conceptualization, Triangulation, Accommodation, Internalization, Externalization, Reconceptualization, Transformation, and Configuration. Through the performance of these stages, all necessary requirements are set in place to encourage intended behavioral change in a governmental system. The template serves as a practical guideline to organize governmental learning events. It submits general directions on how to design a learning process and is therefore applicable to any type of governmental learning event.

The didactic concept of the Learning Spiral is based on an analysis of experiences of how governments learn, the particular knowledge they learn, and how knowledge gets created and transferred to the learning actors. It further takes into account particularities of different governmental models; contemporary theories of policy analysis, political history, and pedagogy; as well as individual, organizational, and governmental learning concepts. The practical application of the eight stages involves an elaborate process that includes the planning, design, and follow-up activities of a particular learning event. The Learning Spiral also takes into account the political environment where the event is taking place, and it requires a deliberate selection of individual learning actors and the governmental and nongovernmental institutions involved.

In summary, the concept of the Learning Spiral focuses not only on the *content* to be learned but—equally important—also on the *process* of how it has to be learned. It provides a theory-guided and practice-approved comprehensive template for how to organize the operations and procedures of effective learning events for governments in the 21st century.

1.3 Outline of the Book

The Black Box of Governmental Learning is structured to address a broad range of interest groups. It is divided into two basic parts: Part I, which consists of chapters 2–4, is directed to an audience that is interested in the analytical and theoretical considerations as well as the methodological development of the Learning Spiral template. Part II is composed of chapters 5–9; it addresses practitioners who want to know how the template is practically applied in different types of governmental learning events. The book concludes with a final chapter, which critically validates and discusses the Learning Spiral in regard to its future development.

Chapter 2: There is no comprehensive description of how governments have learned over time. To address this, chapter 2 gives a short overview of how the principles, tasks, and responsibilities of democratic governments evolved. It also presents a narrative of the various learning approaches that mirror the different historical eras since the beginning of the modern state. This review includes a critical analysis of these approaches from today's perspective, as well as their further developments to meet future requirements.

Besides these historical considerations, the practice of contemporary learning events is examined in regard to design, content, selection of participants, and forms of communication. Based on these critical elements, a selection of worldwide well-known governmental events such as the early G-6—today known as the G-8—conferences, the Mont Fleur Scenario Project in South Africa, and the World Bank's Communities of Practice networks are analyzed to draw on a set of particularities and lessons to be learned.

Chapter 3: Besides the analytical considerations, the concept of the Learning Spiral must further reflect the existing theories related to learning in governments. This chapter starts with a theory-based description of the basic terms of democratic government (learning actor), democratic governance (learning content), and governmental learning (learning activity). *The Black Box of Governmental Learning* considers knowledge in democratic governance as the content governments are expected to learn. Because of its elusive and fast-changing nature, this type of knowledge is carefully analyzed in this chapter regarding its impact on the learning procedure, which is no longer a one-time activity but requires an ongoing process. To further determine the operations and procedures of the learning concept from a didactical and pedagogical perspective also requires the consideration and integration of the major existing individual and organizational learning theories.

Chapter 4: In this chapter, governmental leaning is described as a comprehensive system and the concept of the Learning Spiral is set out as the process that enhances the practical implementation of the knowledge to be learned in a particular political environment. To conceptualize that learning process, the first two chapters are systematically reviewed in regard to concrete subject matter that feeds into the learning process, which is composed of eight stages. To make the learning concept operational, these stages are organized in a template that is applicable to any type of governmental learning event. To ensure the further improvement of the Learning Spiral, a results framework is developed for the Learning Spiral that is designed to measure the overall impact of the application of the learning process.

Chapters 5–9: The Learning Spiral is a generic template that is applied case by case to the circumstances of a specific governmental learning setting. To illustrate how the Learning Spiral can be practically implemented, each of the five chapters in the second part of the book presents a case study representing a different type of event.

These activities are as follows:

1. The 2002 International Conference on Federalism, organized by the Swiss federal and cantonal governments and the International Students Committee, with 600 participants from 60 countries
2. The Global Dialogue Roundtables, a global multiyear program on learning about federal governance, organized by the International Association of Centers of Federal Studies and the Forum of Federations, starting in 2003, with 100 national and international roundtables and more than 2,000 participants from 20 countries

3. A one-week study tour, organized in 2008, on second chamber and judiciary systems from eight countries, with the participation of 20 high-level Iraqi officials representing a post-conflict government
4. A 2008 evaluation-based workshop on public sector reform and decentralization, organized under the lead of the World Bank's Independent Evaluation Group, with 70 participants from 10 African countries
5. A global multimedia training and e-learning initiative about private-public partnerships in infrastructure, spearheaded by the Asian Development Bank Institute, the World Bank Institute, and the Multilateral Investment Fund of the Inter-American Development Bank.

For further illustration, each of these case studies is supplemented by a first-hand account from a participant. These testimonials include statements from the former Premier of Ontario, who is now a current member of the Parliament of Canada; the Deputy Chief Financial Officer and Chief Economist of the Washington, DC, government, the former president of Switzerland; the Chief Justice of the Iraqi Supreme Court; the Head of the Planning and Programming Department of the Ethiopian Ministry of Capacity Building; and the Lead Economist on Public-Private Partnerships from the World Bank Institute.

Chapter 10: The concept of the Learning Spiral is a work in progress. It has to be continuously reviewed and adapted to changes in the practice of learning in democratic governance and new findings in evaluations and research about learning in governments. The final chapter therefore summarizes and reviews the Learning Spiral regarding potential further developments that make it responsive to future global trends and challenges in governmental learning.

Part I: Analytical and Theoretical Considerations

The Learning Spiral emerged out of a dynamic development, which was based on analytical and theoretical concepts as well as their practical application over the last decade. Whenever the review of the practical use of the Learning Spiral detected insufficiencies or requested improvements, it was further developed based on the latest available theories; it was then reapplied in a subsequent governmental learning event. Thus, many different analytical and theoretical concepts were considered and built into the Learning Spiral over the years. Part I describes first the analytical concepts (chapter 2) and second the theoretical concepts (chapter 3) that were used to develop this new process for governmental learning as it exists to date (chapter 4).

2 Analytical Concepts of Governmental Learning

Governmental learning is a multidimensional and complex subject that needs to be carefully analyzed and reviewed in regard to its past (see section 2.1) and current experiences (see section 2.2). Such an analysis will allow a better understanding of the different approaches and particularities of governmental learning in today's practice and may explain and/or contradict the widespread impression that democratic governments do not learn (see section 2.3). This examination will demonstrate that learning in governments represents a unique and distinctive understanding that goes beyond conventional individual and/or organizational learning.

2.1 Historical Analysis

In the history of the modern state, as of today no comprehensive description exists of how governments in either developed or developing countries have learned. Despite this lack of empirical evidence, there is a common belief that governments evolved over time and therefore consciously or unconsciously were in a state of learning, to improve their capacity to stay in power and/or to improve public services and public goods delivered to people (Kemp and Weehuizen 2005).

Important insights can be gained from analyzing developments in governance over time if historical contexts are included in the analysis (Herbst 2000; Batterbury and Fernando 2006). To derive a proximate overview of the practices of *governmental learning*[1] over time, a brief analysis will present a set of different approaches that mirror the various historical eras of learning in governments since the beginning of the modern state.

---

1. The term *governmental learning* was initially introduced in the scientific literature by Etheredge (1981) and will be further elaborated in subsection 3.1.2.

2.1.1 Origins

The earliest forms of *government*, which go back to ancient Greece, the Roman Republic, and other previous empires, emerged when it became possible to centralize power in a sustainable way.[2] This implies that a government concentrates power in a single head or center, and the government itself can be controlled and its environment managed. Where people did not fit into that set-up, the government tried to force them into it, or they were simply expelled or displaced outside the state boundaries. Governments in these early times were mostly monarchies or oligarchies led by an individual or a few who were backed by a ruling class. The often-impoverished population did not have any political say and had little means to influence governments or to pressure them for change. As a consequence, government leaders had no real incentives to review or change the function of the state. Learning in this context was basically reduced to improving strategies that would ensure the survival of the existing political system (Finer 1997).

With the discovery of the New World in the 15th century, the inadequacies of the monarchal government model began to be clear, and after a series of modern revolutions in Europe and its colonies—in particular in the British colonies and France—new liberal and democratic principles emerged.[3] They were based on the understanding that all men are created equal and that certain inalienable rights such as life, liberty, and the pursuit of happiness endow them. It became citizens' expectation that governments would secure these rights, as they derived their powers from the consent of the governed.[4]

This consent of the governed became the key to governmental legitimacy. According to Max Weber's influential definition, governments came to be seen as the political institution that had a monopoly on the legitimate use of physical and legal power within a given territory. These powers include the armed forces, civil service or state bureaucracy,

---

2. For today's understanding of the term *government*, see subsection 3.1.1, which describes contemporary concepts of governments in the era of the modern state.
3. These modern revolutions were based on and expressed by liberal thinkers such as Hobbes, Spinoza, Locke, and Rousseau.
4. See, for example, the U.S. Declaration of Independence.

courts, and the police. In return, the government is expected to take care of its citizens in matters of social and political services (Weber 1921).

These early assignments of government responsibility in the modern state developed slowly and haltingly over time toward a broad political agenda of fully institutionalized democracies, professional bureaucracies, rules for corporate governance, modern financial institutions, extensive social welfare services, and so on. The content of this emerging and continuously growing agenda of governmental institutions and liabilities, today called principles of democratic governance, was the result of experience and the advocacy of committed citizens, interest groups, scholars, and so forth, which were dedicated to further a new understanding of the fundamentals in the modern state (Grindle 2004).

The formation and incorporation of these aspects of democratic governance in today's developed countries took centuries, and this process is still not fully accomplished (Grindle 2004). This may be even more the case for developing countries, in which the process of state building and democratization began after they gained independence in the middle of the 20th century. In many cases these countries copied the models from the previous colonizing states, which most often proved unsuitable for the needs of newly created states. The apparent gulf between the developed and developing countries, as well as the inadequacy of the aspects of democratic governance they applied, made the developing states appear slow and far behind in the process of becoming full-fledged democratic countries.[5]

This trend of slow implementation of principles of democratic governance has not changed much over the last decade despite the growing impact of globalization. This development emerged with the fall of the Iron Curtain in Europe in the late 1980s and was accelerated with information technology in the last 20 years.[6] With globalization, the ideological bias between the communist system in the *East* and the capitalist system

---

5. For a comparison of states in regard to the quality of their democratic governance system over time, see Daniel Kaufmann et al. (2009).
6. Others consider the breakup of the Soviet Union as the decisive historical event that marked the change from a bipolar to a unipolar world and triggered the process of globalization (Raskin et al. 2002; World Bank 2008).

in the *West* lost its influence[7] and was replaced by the concept of the free global market, enhanced by easier access to digitalized information.[8]

One of the political results of this enormous macroeconomical shift was growing expectations of citizens and societal interest groups for more political freedom, participatory and sustainable development, and universal human rights. This fundamental political change resulted in an overwhelming increase of the quantity, differentiation, and complexity of the different aspects of democratic governance (Hubbard 1999; Punyaratabandhy 2004). The 1997 World Development Report sets the number of aspects of democratic governance at 45 (World Bank 1997). By 2002 the list had grown to 116 items (Grindle 2004).

As a consequence, the democratic governance agenda evolved into a life-spanning concept of governmental activities, which was becoming hard to oversee. An analysis of this growth of principles, tasks, and responsibilities shows that the term of democratic governance to date has no standard meaning; no doubt new elements will be added and possibly old ones will be dropped in the future (Doornbos 2003).

However, without being exhaustive a broad understanding of democratic governance embraces basically the following elements:[9] democratic governance consists of the distribution of power among institutions of government. It includes the legitimacy and authority of state institutions; rules and norms that determine who holds power and how decisions are made about the exercise of authority; relationships of accountability among state officials and between these officials and citizens; the ability to make policy, manage the administrative and fiscal affairs of the state, and deliver public services and public goods that match citizens' preferences and needs; and the impact of institutions and policies on public welfare and human rights.

---

7. This distinction between colonizing and colonized excludes the so-called group of block-free states, which during the Cold War tried to develop a unique and independent type of governance. Overall, these attempts had limited impact and will therefore not be further discussed.
8. At this time, economists and business thinkers were describing the birth of a global economy, where knowledge was outstripping material resources and capital as a source of wealth (Willke 1993).
9. For a comprehensive theoretical definition of the term democratic governance, see subsection 3.1.1.

Because of the overwhelming and overarching number and complexity of the given agenda of democratic governance, governments were increasingly faced with crucial decisions about setting priorities in regard to which elements of that agenda should be applied first and which should follow, what is essential and what is not, what could be achieved in the short term and what over the longer term, as well as what is feasible and what is not (Grindle 2004).

The challenges for developing countries in learning how to answer these questions became even stronger with the *Washington Consensus* and the good governance agenda.[10] This agreement, introduced by the international donor and development community in the early 1980s, demanded that developing countries comply with all major principles of democratic governance at once without considering their particular cultural, economical, political, or social circumstances. If the developing countries failed to comply, the conditions for getting loans and credits became restricted or denied.

Tackling these enormous external pressures and simultaneously moving ahead in the democratization process required an enormous effort to build and leverage learning capacities in democratic governance. Developing countries had not only to learn how to incorporate basic democratic principles but to do so in the shortest possible time and by setting the right priorities and determining which principles, tasks, and responsibilities to consider first and which ones later on (Graham et al. 2003).

It is therefore safe to say that in the era of globalization, in the last two decades, the ability of governments to learn has become the most critical factor in successfully implementing the democratic governance agenda. To develop, absorb, and implement the latest and adequate experiences and knowledge in democratic governance was recognized as the best way to improve governmental capacities to match citizens' expectations; for developing countries, this was also the way to reduce poverty and achieve sustainable growth (World Bank 2008).

---

10. The term *Washington Consensus* was initially introduced 1989 by John Williamson to describe a set of 10 specific economic policy prescriptions that he considered should constitute the standard reform package promoted for crisis-wracked developing countries by Washington, DC-based institutions such as the International Monetary Fund, the World Bank, and the US Treasury Department (see Williamson 1989).

2.1.2 Learning Approaches

In one way or another, democratic governments have been learning for centuries. However, over time they adopted different learning approaches with different purposes, depending on the circumstances they faced. With the beginning of the modern state, today's developed countries adopted, altered, and replaced their principles, tasks, and responsibilities of democratic governance in an ongoing struggle, in which they wrestled over the right number, the right sequence, the right mix, and the right content of the elements of such a comprehensive governance agenda. From a learning perspective, this struggle over time can be labeled *learning by doing* or *learning by using* (Kemp and Weehuizen 2005; see also Table 1). According to this approach, governments selected and applied measures to improve their democratic governance model and—depending their success or failure—revised or changed them for new and more promising interventions.

This established more or less successful learning-by-doing approach stands in sharp contrast to the governmental learning concepts observed since the middle of the 20th century in many of today's developing countries. In the course of decolonization, emerging states in Africa and Asia were expected to develop their governmental models from scratch and overnight. To be able to do this, they were expected to copy and learn

Table 1 Historic Approaches to Learning in Democratic Governments

Developed countries	Developing countries	Globalized world
French and American Revolution, since late 18th Century	Decolonization in Asia and Africa, since mid-20th Century	Fall of Iron Curtain in Europe, since end of 20th Century
Development of principles of democratic governance	Application of a normative set of principles of democratic governance	Situational application of selected principles of democratic governance
Over time	On time	Sequencing
Learning by doing	Learning from others	Learning from each other

from the experiences of developed countries. This so-called North-South learning took place regardless of any cultural, economic, historical, geographic, and social differences (Blunt 1995).

The underlying perspective of this learning approach can be called *learning from others* or in slightly less provocative terms *learning by observing* (Kemp and Weehuizen 2005; see also Table 1). Based on this approach, countries were expected to adopt a democratic governance model from other countries in a one-time move, regardless of their different situational and contextual factors.

This approach of learning from others was mainly applied by developing countries. However, an overview of measurements of how governments of these countries performed during the last decade shows little evidence that this learning approach considerably improved the quality of democratic governance (Santiso 2001).[11] The following three arguments underline this perception (Grindle 2004; Andrews 2008a, 2010):

1. Developed countries evolved inconsistently and heterogeneously. History has shown that regarding the implementation of principles, tasks, and responsibilities of democratic governance, there is no *one-size-fits-all* approach. Depending on the circumstances in a particular country or region, there are different ways that these principles might work. Thus, in the rationale of the *cultural relativism*[12] concept, what is working well in one country might not necessarily be successful in another, and what might be right in a certain period might not be right in another.

---

11. For more detailed information about the measurement of democratic governance, see the World Bank Institute's governance performance indicators (Kaufmann et al. 2009). Other selected measurements come to similar conclusions: Assessment Methodology for Public Procurements Systems of the OECD, the Country Policy and Institutional Assessment, the Development Program's Human Development Index of the UN, the Global Integrity Index, the Millennium Challenge Account of the U.S. government, the Public Expenditure and Financial Accountability Assessment, the Open Budget Index, the Transparency International ranking system, as well as the World Development Indicators of the World Bank. For a critical overview of such measurements and country rankings, see Rotberg (2004/05).
12. The concept of *cultural relativism* is documented by empirical research that has proven that perceptions of what constitutes the principle of political participation, as well as views concerning its desirability, attitudes toward authority, uncertainty, group versus individual loyalties, varies between different cultures (Blunt 1995).

2. Developed countries incorporated different principles in different stages over time. Thus it is not reasonable to expect that emerging states can implement the whole agenda of governmental principles, tasks, and responsibilities at once or in a short period. The controversial issue is therefore less whether developing countries shall or shall not implement these principles, tasks, and responsibilities than it is in what time frame they shall be applied and how.

3. The process of introducing a democratic governmental model became more difficult with the growing number of principles, tasks, and responsibilities resulting from the growing impact of globalization. The pressure to incorporate these new and equally important elements of a comprehensive governance agenda forced governments to make choices between the essential and the desirable and between changes that can be instrumented in the short term and those that take longer to emerge and produce benefits.

Considering these arguments, the implementation of appropriate principles, tasks, and responsibilities in a governmental model depends on different factors, such as the circumstances a country is facing, the timing in which these elements of a comprehensive governance agenda have to be implemented, and what a government's priorities are. These variables point out that there is no reliable normative knowledge to guarantees the successful development of a democratic government.[13] Despite this conclusion, the democratization agenda continued to grow in size and complexity, and so did the pressure on developing countries to incorporate these principles, tasks, and responsibilities without any consideration of context, timing, or prioritization.

Faced with that dilemma, developing countries are beginning to look for alternative approaches that would allow them to become independent from the extant models of developed countries and instead give them the freedom to turn to each other's experiences. In this so-called South-South learning concept, governments are developing their policy actions relying on the successes and failures of other developing countries that have a comparable degree of development and that are dealing

---

13. Batterbury and Fernando (2006) arrive at the same conclusion. They introduce a collection of papers that provides empirical studies of the impacts of changes in established modes of governance.

with similar problems and conditions. This approach can be described as *learning from each other* or *learning by interacting* (Kemp and Weehuizen 2005; see also Table 1). It is based on the assumption that governments are prepared to share each other's experiences and act as equal partners in an open and transparent manner. The approach only works, however, when all parties are ready to follow these *rules* without any preconditions or hidden agendas.

There is good reason to believe that this approach of learning from each other is not limited to developing countries alone but could be easily expanded to developed countries, for instance, in the global financial crisis, which to different degrees has reached almost every country in the last two years. There are no solutions yet to solve this crisis effectively. Thus, it appears reasonable and obvious that all affected countries could agree to share their experiences to find common solutions, which subsequently will be applied according to each country's individual needs. Following this north-east-south-west learning concept, there are no limits in regard to potential sources of knowledge, regardless of whether they are coming from developed or developing countries. Such universal and unlimited knowledge exchanges allow the comparison of best practices and experiences, which may lead to new and unknown solutions.

Table 1 shows an overview of the three distinctive governmental learning approaches that emerged over time. Their first appearance always occurred with an historical event, which forced governments to develop new ways of learning. They emerged in the past and still have relevance in today's governmental learning. However, it is expected that with the emergence of future historical challenges and incidents, new approaches will appear and may replace or further develop the existing models of learning in democratic governments.

2.2 Today's Practices

Today, learning in governments has expanded to a broad and fast-growing industry. However, its current approaches and methods are still heavily rooted in past experiences and, as will be shown, the actual practices of governmental learning allow the derivation of a wide range of lessons to be learned, which may lead—if taken seriously—to a significant increase in the quality of democratic governance.

2.2.1 Learning Approaches Today

Today all three approaches of governmental learning are common. However, they have different appearances and frequencies and have developed and improved to meet the challenges of today's domestic and global problems. The most frequently used approaches are still learning by doing and learning from others, but increasingly learning from each other can be seen. It is used particularly in cases where governments are forced to deal with cross-border challenges like the financial crisis, pandemics, climate change, and so forth, and therefore rely on international comparative experiences.

Learning by doing is perhaps still the most prevalent governmental learning approach in developed countries. Despite the drawbacks related to this costly *trial-and-error* approach, the majority of today's developed countries continuously increased their overall governmental performance over time (Kaufmann et al. 2009). One explanation for this paradox is that since the late 1960s developed countries introduced elaborate evidence-based evaluation concepts that allowed them to significantly improve the quality of their decisions about democratic governance.[14]

The increasingly sophisticated and refined instruments of performance measurement and evaluation allow a systematic and targeted review of past accomplishments in democratic governance. By using performance measurement and evaluation, governments are able to develop and improve their decisions about future democratic governance strategies by avoiding past failures and mistakes. A major side effect of these evaluations is that they also serve as accountability measures, so the public can learn about the performance of governments in a relatively independent manner. The better the public is informed about past practices, the more citizens have a chance to get actively involved in the governmental decision-making process.[15]

---

14. Under the pressure of continuous public concerns about governments performing their duties and responsibilities, governments in developed countries established and incorporated a variety of different kinds of internal and external evaluation units. Among them were auditor offices, internal and external evaluation, monitoring and controlling units, and so forth (Rist 1994).

15. See in this context also the concept of the *policy cycle,* according to which govern-

In developed countries the introduction of evidence-based evaluations in the political decision-making process certainly helped straighten out the most evident disadvantages of the learning-by-doing approach. It also appears that, as a consequence of this, learning by doing became more attractive in developing countries, too. Many of them are currently in the process of building up their evidence-based evaluation capacities. They are getting strong support from international development organizations, in particular the World Bank. These organizations are introducing broad monitoring and evaluation programs in their client countries with the goal of improving the overall democratic governance performance.[16]

Nonetheless, today's practices show that the international donor community still expects governments from developing countries to follow the learning-from-others approach. The fundamentals of this approach are based in the belief that there is an objective and empirically proven set of normative knowledge, essentially generated in developed countries, that determines how to develop and maintain an efficient and effective democratic governance model. That community assumes that this knowledge can be transmitted in a one-time or at least short effort from the ones that know it to the ones that do not. The pressure in developing countries is therefore high to incorporate the full agenda of principles of democratic governance at once and in the shortest possible timeframe (Hoebink 2006).

From this perspective, the democratic governance model is seen merely as a condition instead of a process toward a successfully functioning democratic governance setting. To reinforce this approach international and regional development banks introduced the *concept of conditionalities* as structural adjustment programs following the debt

---

ments adapt their policies to past experiences and expected future challenges in a structured way of policy formulation, implementation, and accountability (see Leeuw and Sonnichsen 1994).

16. See, for example, the Regional Centers for Learning on Evaluation and Results (CLEAR), launched by the World Bank's Independent Evaluation Group. The program is a collaborative effort among donors and partner countries to strengthen the monitoring and evaluation capacity of partner countries (see http://www.worldbank.org/ieg/clear/).

crisis of the 1980s.[17] According to this approach, client countries were required to fulfill the criteria of democratic governance before they would become eligible for loans, debt relief, and/or financial aid (Koeberle et al. 2005).

Despite these reinforcing measures, learning from others does not appear to fully meet the expectations set in this approach so far. The sole focus on the given normative agenda leads to governmental behavior that ignores situational and country specific criteria (see subsection 2.1.2). In practice, governments tend to be overwhelmed by the magnitude of expected governmental action. Confronted with the reality that not all measures can be implemented at once, and under the pressure of the concept of conditionality, governments are inclined to concentrate primarily on observable and preferred (by the donor community) governmental outcomes and neglect tacit and hard-to-measure tasks. Furthermore, the lack of ownership in regard to the imposed measures lowers the motivation and undermines the confidence that the given normative political actions are the right and only ones that will improve government performance.

To balance the negative interference of the learning-from-others approach, governments—in particular from middle-income countries—are becoming more cautious about which principles, tasks, and responsibilities of democratic governance they want to implement and in what order. They are beginning on a case-by-case process to split up the given normative model into its respective parts and to transform them so they appear to best serve their specific situation. Experiences so far demonstrated that in general, such prioritized items showed visible improvements, whereas those that were not prioritized ended up, at least temporarily, to be neglected. Practice in the future will show if these deferred items will be pursued with the same engagement once the previous ones are successfully implemented.

Finally, learning from each other appears to be the least frequently used approach. Practice shows that governments of developed and

---

17. See *Review of World Bank Conditionality* (World Bank 2005). In general terms this concept is based on the framework of the Rational Choice Theory, according to which individuals tend to choose the best action to stable preference functions and constraints that are facing them (Dunleavy 1991).

developing countries tend to be hesitant about sharing their practices with each other. Among the reasons is the disbelief that other government experiences could be a valuable source of knowledge in solving their specific domestic problems. Another reason lies in the ongoing competition between countries. They do not want to give up potential competitive advantages and therefore hold back their valuable experiences. And last, some governments may hide their past practices in order to not openly admit potentially unsuccessful political actions.

To make learning from each other more attractive for today's governments, some clarifications need therefore to be understood:

1. Participation in such an approach is voluntary. Different experiences have to be understood as a source of inspiration for alternative problem solving. Governments are free to decide whether and in what form these new insights could be used in their practical governmental activities. There is no assumption or expectation that they will be relevant on an operational level.

2. At first glance, learning from each other does not work in a competitive environment. The approach requires that all governments that want to be involved in this learning process be committed to sharing their experiences in partnership and among equals. Only if they do so collectively will they in return get to know others' experiences and possibly learn how to improve their own model. In this sense, governments that are involved in such a learning approach will almost certainly enhance their performance in democratic governance.

3. In view of the complexity and universality of global problems and the difficulty of hiding their difficulties in dealing with them, governments must overcome their reservations toward the mutual learning process. Contributions about failed policies in governmental learning are just as valuable as successful experiences are. "We can learn not only from the successes but also from the failures of states and of the mechanisms and processes they have employed to deal with problems" (Watts 2008).[18]

---

18. Watts (2008) makes this conclusion in reference to federal states. However, it is the opinion of the author that this statement is perfectly applicable for other governmental models, too.

4. As much as the principles, tasks, and responsibilities in democratic governance are changing, expanding, and becoming more complex, learning from each other has to be seen as a never-ending process, too. This learning approach is an iterative process that is continually repeated.

To make learning from each other an attractive approach for governments, the practical learning methodology has to address the problems and concerns elaborated here. Its practical application has to establish a knowledge-sharing dynamic, which is based on confidentiality, mutuality, noncompetitiveness, inclusiveness, partnership, truthfulness, and willingness. Governments have to be fully aware of these obligations as well as the advantages and disadvantages of the potential gains of the process (Blindenbacher and Saunders 2005).

2.2.2 Practical Application

The practical application of the three learning approaches can take place in all kinds of formal as well as informal settings. The latter may be the rule and the former the exception. Governments—in particular those in developed countries—that primarily followed the learning-by-doing approach in the past appeared to learn outside established and targeted learning events. Learning in these cases seemed to be coincidental and unpredictable. It is difficult to get an overview of these informal learning activities, and they are not much reflected in the contemporary literature. Unlike with informal learning, there is growing attention on formal and prearranged learning in governments (see subsection 3.1.2). This may be in large part related to the historical developments since the middle of the last century, where learning from others became the leading learning approach in many developing countries and evoked a strong interest for conscious and well-structured learning concepts.

Most of these kinds of formal governmental learning take place at events like conferences, e-learning activities, roundtables, study tours, training sessions, or workshops. These prearranged activities, which usually follow a formal agenda and are set up to give participants the opportunity to exchange their views about matters of common concern, exist in all shapes and sizes. Participants number from a few individuals to several thousand participants. The existing designs of these events vary a lot, too; however, the predominant event type is shaped by one-way communication with typically four different kinds of role takers:[19] first, the event organizer, who is responsible for the logistics and selects the event topic;[20] second, the moderator, who facilitates the event sessions and assures the compliance of the agenda; third, the speakers, the so-called knowledge holders or transmitters; and fourth, the audience, the knowledge seekers or recipients.

These types of learning events are based on the assumption that there is information or knowledge that is relevant to a particular subject and therefore attracts an audience that is either self-selected or chosen by the organizer.[21] Usually the speaker is known as an expert on the subject and represents the major single perspective on the issue at stake and has the capacity to present it in a comprehensive and conclusive manner. To make the event more lively and therefore more attractive, the organizers often invite two or more speakers with opposite points of view to provoke controversy and by doing so launch a debate. By listening to the discussions, the participants get the opportunity either to take sides or to search for common ground between the presented positions. In any case, this event model is based on the assumption that there exists a collective interest of an audience that wants to listen to the different perspectives of one or more experts on the given subject.

In the learning events described above, it is common to have little time reserved for the audience to get involved and to share reflections or give feedback that allows any further development of the presented knowledge. In general, most of the available time is used for the presentations, and further interactions are usually reserved for the official speaker or speakers, who are already on stage. In most cases, audience engagement is limited to asking questions of the presenters about the particular content of their speeches. As a convention as well as a courtesy toward the speakers and organizers of the event, variances from the given agenda seldom occur, and if they do, the moderator is expected

---

19. This kind of formal one-way communication type of adult learning accounts for over seventy percent of all delivered learning hours (Goldstein and Ford 2002; Sugrue and Kim 2004).
20. Today it is common practice for the logistical organization of conferences with high attendance to be outsourced to specialized event enterprises.
21. The distinction of the terms *information* and *knowledge* will be further defined (see subsection 3.2.1).

to intervene and to redirect the flow of communication to the original topic at stake.

This organized form of interaction is in technical terms called *discussion*. By definition, the participants in a discussion know beforehand everything they think needs to be known about the subject at hand and therefore they also know all relevant answers. The main purpose of such an interaction is to exchange different viewpoints. If a particular argument appears to be weak or invalid, the discussants will replace it with a better one to become more persuasive in future discussions (Schein 1998).

In a discussion-oriented learning event, all interactions other than the formal exchange of arguments are held in informal settings, such as coffee breaks or lunches. The disadvantage of this form of communication is that it is fruitful only for the individuals who are directly involved. The other participants at the learning event who are not involved in these spontaneous and coincidental encounters are excluded from such interactions, even though the content may be important to them, too. As a consequence, the learning effect of such a communication model lies to a high degree in the quality of the speaker's expertise as well as his or her didactical and communicative skills. The more a speaker or knowledge provider is able to anticipate the potential participants' interests and subsequently adapt the content and form of his or her speech, the likelier it is that the presentation will have an impact on the audience's or the knowledge seekers' ways of thinking and acting later on.

To improve the quality of this kind of presentation, there exists a whole industry of coaches and teachers that provide specialized courses and training in rhetorical skills as well as the use of all sorts of technical appliances.[22] Though it is hard to verify the concrete impact of presentation techniques and technical support in learning events, they are without doubt based on the intention of improving the quality of such activities. However, despite these efforts, empirical evidence proves they have not necessarily translated into measurable results. For example, an evaluation of the World Bank's project-based training events concludes that only half of the Bank-financed training "resulted in substantial changes to work place behavior or enhance development capacity" (IEG 2008a). This conclusion stands in

---

22. Such technical support instruments are audio and video equipment, electronic flipcharts, overhead projectors, PowerPoint® etc. For a complete overview of technical appliances as well as rhetorical techniques, see ADB (2009).

sharp contrast to the financial efforts invested into the form and organization of governmental learning events over the past years.[23]

Besides these findings of the limited effect of governmental learning events to date, governments are increasingly challenged in their learning capacities by the consequences of globalization. Through globalization, the already complex agenda in knowledge in democratic governance is becoming more elusive and fast changing.[24] Governments are finding it increasingly difficult to identify the appropriate knowledge they need to properly handle their challenges, even though today's information technology provides more information about democratic governance than ever before. There appears to be a trend that shows societies in general and governments in particular are overwhelmed by the vast amount of information on any given subject. Therefore, they have to rely increasingly on the knowledge and expertise of experts to find the relevant solutions to tackle their given societal and political challenges (Willke 1993). Developing countries in particular seem to be affected by these developments, which makes their struggle to reach development goals look harder and more ambitious.

However, the dichotomy between available and needed information as the basis for better decision making in democratic governance is a challenge not only for the policy actors but also for the experts, and for the speakers in governmental learning events as well. Like anybody else, they are challenged by the difficult task of distinguishing between relevant and irrelevant information. They are expected to make that distinction before anybody else does so they can present new and exclusive conclusions to their potential audiences.

Taking note of the challenges in this globalized world, particularly for developing countries, as well as recognizing the limited impact of governmental learning events to date, the World Bank Group launched a major global knowledge sharing initiative in the mid-1990s.[25] This initiative is

---

23. The World Bank invests an estimated $720 million annually in support of client training (IEG 2008a).
24. The issue of how knowledge in democratic governance is growing over time in the era of globalization is described in subsection 2.1.1 and how it is created and analyzed in section 3.2.
25. World Bank President James Wolfensohn launched the Global Knowledge Learning Initiative at his Annual Meeting address in October 1996. For further information, see the World Development Report *Knowledge for Development* (World Bank 1998).

based on the belief that knowledge in democratic governance is a key factor for poverty reduction and sustainable development. Over time it became a model for expanded knowledge sharing activities and knowledge management in international and regional donor and development organizations worldwide (King and McGrath 2002).

One of the main objectives of this knowledge management agenda is to enhance the capacity of client countries to meet their development goals as formulated in the MDGs (World Bank 1998). Accessibility and delivery of information alone was no longer seen as sufficient. Instead, the World Bank promoted the development of new concepts of knowledge management that helps governments enhance their own capacities to select, adopt, and apply newly acquired knowledge.

Taking heed of global developments, the World Bank triggered a world-embracing movement to search for and create new concepts of knowledge sharing. These emerging types of learning events designed for governments were based on a critical analysis of past learning concepts (Mackay 1998; Perrin and Mackay 1999) as well as on newly developed alternative models, which in many ways were based on the approach of learning from each other (see subsection 2.1.2). Among the many concepts were appreciative inquiry, coalition building, focus groups, open space and scenario planning events, peer-to-peer learning, and so forth.[26] Many of the applied learning activities were blended and included different methods, techniques, and resources in the same learning activity (Graham 2005).

An overview of these new types of learning events shows that they vary greatly in form and purpose. However, they all share common characteristics and rules of communication, which significantly differ from conventional learning events. First and most important, there are no more designated speakers who are expected to be subject matter experts per se. The main actors of the event are now all involved individuals. Every participant is considered an active contributor. Everyone is expected to be prepared to share his or her experiences as transpar-

---

Similar knowledge and learning initiatives were also launched by the British Council, the Leland Initiative from USAID, and UNDP (Digital 4Sight 2002).

26. These are a selection of different types of learning events in current use at the World Bank Institute (WBI). WBI is the capacity development arm of the World Bank and helps countries share and apply global and local knowledge to meet development challenges (WBI 2009).

ently and openly as possible, whenever it appears reasonable and helpful to move the process of learning forward. As a result, each participant pays his or her admission in a figurative way to participate. Although everybody is expected to do this, the reward for the individual learning actor will be unlimited access to the collective shared knowledge.

The agendas of such learning activities tend to be open and leave space for change if it becomes necessary. The activities commonly include three distinctive roles. First is the event organizer. In close collaboration with the potential participants, this actor defines the event content and takes care of the conference logistics. Second are the learning actors, who are expected to be knowledge transmitters and recipients alike. Third, the moderator oversees and leads the process and reinforces the communication rules such as equality, reciprocity, openness, and impartiality.[27] His or her main task is to ensure that all participants who are willing to share their experiences and opinions are explicitly invited to do so and therefore have a fair chance to take part in the event proceedings. This stands in contrast to the role of a moderator in the conventional learning concept. In that model, the moderator is expected to ensure that the audience respects the course of a given agenda, which gives speakers the space for their presentations and limits the role of the audience to listening and occasionally asking questions.

This form of interaction is called a *dialogue*. Based on the theory of group dynamics, dialogue is a type of formalized communication in which participants do not pretend to know an issue in all its aspects or the solutions to the problems related to it. However, they have an idea of the complexity of the problem and are aware of what they know and what they do not know. By participating in the learning process, they hope that other participants will deliver complementary knowledge and thus help to find new solutions that each participant alone may not have found (Isaacs 1999; Schein 2004).

2.2.3 Types of Events

Most of today's learning events focus either on individual participants or on entire organizations. There are numerous examples for each type of

---

27. These communication rules are closely related to the ones developed by Juergen Habermas (1987a, 1987b) in his *theory of communicative action*. For the practical application of these rules, see also Blindenbacher (1999).

governmental learning event. One of the many, but presumably the best-known, governmental learning events that focus on individual learning is the annual Group of Six (G-6) conferences.[28] As originally designed in the mid-1970s, the three-day conferences were a typical peer-to-peer event that assembled the heads of government or the heads of state from the world's six—today eight—most industrialized democracies. The annual roundtables were a gathering of equals with no designated leader. The event rules foresaw that each participant was allowed to present one item for the agenda, and the last conference session deliberately had no agenda at all. The roundtable was not supposed to be the place where the details of difficult or controversial policy issues had to be fleshed out. The purpose was not to dream up quick fixes, but to talk and think about them together (Bayne and Putnam 2000).

There are just as many events that focus on governmental institutions as there are that primarily relate to individual policy actors. Events most often take place in intergovernmental settings, where different interdependent orders of government consult, cooperate, coordinate, and negotiate their policies to solve conflicts or to adapt to changing circumstances. These learning events usually take the form of standing—most of the time annual—meetings involving ministers, legislators, officials, and agencies of different national or subnational governments (Watts 2008). An important feature of these events is that the participants represent a particular institutional unit, which is relevant for the topic at hand. It is expected that the individual who represents a unit is its leader or primary stakeholder. This ensures that the counterparts in such events are from the same hierarchical level and represent, from an organizational point of view, the same perspective.[29]

Another learning event that focuses on the institutions in a given country is the Mont Fleur scenario. This model was undertaken in

---

28. The annual G-6 conferences emerged following the 1973 oil crisis and the subsequent global recession. The first conference was inaugurated by the French President Valery Giscard d'Estaing in France in November 1975. The design of the meetings evolved over time and has become more structured by having a fixed agenda, which is set and convened by the host country. The comments about the event here refer to its original design (Bayne and Putnam 2000).
29. Among the intergovernmental conferences are, for example, the Council of Australian Governments and the Social Union for Canadians (Watts 2008).

South Africa in the early 1990s.[30] Scenario planning is a methodology of approaching and anticipating the future; it is increasingly used as a tool for strategizing in private and public sector organizations (Schoemaker 1995).[31] The Mont Fleur project brought together a diverse group of 22 prominent South African politicians, activists, academics, and businessmen from across the ideological spectrum to think creatively about the future of their country. The individuals had to represent all-important perspectives on the issues determined by the event agenda. They were selected because of their ability to influence their communities or constituencies. However, these individuals did not necessarily need to be the official or elected holder of a position. Under the leadership of publicly well-respected and independent moderators, the participants met three times in a series of three-day workshops. The purpose of the Mont Fleur events was not to present definitive truths, but to stimulate debate on how to shape the next 10 years of the South African state. The principle value of these workshops was to build common ground among different perspectives and parties (Beery et al. 2009).

With no doubt the G-6 conferences and the Mont Fleur project are widely considered as highly successful learning events. However, from a governmental learning perspective their impact could have been even higher would they have equally reflected individual and organizational aspects into the learning process. The G-6 conferences on the one hand were exclusively designed for individual decision makers. The primary learning experience was exclusively directed to the immediate participants and leaves out other important actors, outside the executive units.[32] The

---

30. The Mont Fleur events were held at the conference center outside of Cape Town during 1991 and 1992 (Beery et al. 2009).
31. The scenario process is logical, open, and informal. Building scenarios can be creative because the process is about telling stories, not about making commitments. A story about the future has to be able to encompass all aspects of the world: social, political, economic, cultural, ecological, etc. One of the premises of scenario thinking is that the future is not predetermined and cannot be predicted, which means that the choices we make can influence what happens. A scenario conversation turns the attention of a group away from the past and present toward the future. It shifts from looking for the solution to exploring different possibilities (Schoemaker 1995).
32. Secretary of State Henry Kissinger, unquestionably an important personality in the US administration, accompanied President Gerald Ford to the first G-6 meeting but was denied access to the roundtable because he was not the head of state or head of government (Thatcher 2009).

intergovernmental conferences and the Mont Fleur events, on the other hand, focus primarily on the development of governmental institutions and tend to neglect the individual dimension in the learning process.

Among today's practitioners and experts in the field of governmental learning, there is strong belief that for governments to successfully face the challenges of a globalized world, governmental learning events have to focus equally on individual and organizational learning aspects (Connor and Dovers 2004). If policy actors do not get institutional support to implement newly acquired knowledge, it is almost certain that they will end up abandoning their efforts for change. To increase the impact of governmental learning, such events should therefore go beyond the prevailing two types of learning as presented by the G-6 and Mont Fleur models. To fully optimize both types of learning, both models have to be used simultaneously and in a coordinated manner.

Illustrative and successful examples for this type of integrated learning are *communities of practice* networks.[33] These social networks are self-organized groups of people who share a concern or a passion for something they do and learn together how to do it better in an organizational frame. Participants optimize their sharing and learning from each other's experiences in a sociocultural context. The World Bank and other leading development organizations have found that these communities are an ideal vehicle for dealing with learning and knowledge. This type of learning provides a new approach that focuses on people and on the social structures that enable them to learn with and from each other.[34] This approach of participative knowledge management is directed to improve individual and organizational abilities to spread successful practices; better use existing knowledge assets; and more systematically learn from staff, clients, and partners to enable innovation (Wenger 2006).

---

33. Other types of learning events that consider individual and organizational learning are, for example, the World Bank's Open Governance Initiative (World Bank 2009c) and the Power of Appreciative Inquiry program developed by Diana Whitney (Whitney and Trosten-Bloom 2003).

34. The term *community of practice* is of relatively recent coinage, even though the phenomenon it refers to is very old. Today, there is hardly any sizeable organization in the developing or the developed world that does not have some form of community of practice initiative. The first appearances of the communities of practice in the World Bank go back to the thematic groups, which were established in the frame of the World Bank's knowledge initiative in 1996 (Lave and Wenger 1991; Wenger 1998, 2006, 2008).

In today's practice, learning events reflecting individual as well as organizational considerations such as the communities of practice are still rare. This is certainly the case in the learning operations of the World Bank, one of the world's largest single providers of governmental learning activities. The latest evaluation results that measure the Bank's efforts to build capacity in development effectiveness conclude that most of the Bank-financed learning events resulted in individual participant learning but improved the capacity of client organizations to achieve development objectives only about half the time (IEG 2008a, 2008d).[35] It is suspected that this negative ratio may be no different in other international learning agencies.

The reports generated two further critical results in regard to contemporary governmental learning (IEG 2008a): The first result was a questioning of the theoretically unfounded learning concepts. Most of today's learning events overlook the whole range of pedagogical as well as group dynamic theories, which could serve to inspire the development of effective learning designs. These findings are not necessarily a surprise, because to date the contemporary literature offers few theory-based concepts to enhance participatory and interactive governmental learning. The second result is a questioning of the insufficient attention paid to the particular governmental context in which learning activities take place. Effective learning events have to include professional curriculum designs that match the learning actors and their institutions' cultural, economic, political, and social characteristics.

In summary, these evaluation reports conclude that to organize effective governmental learning events, individual and organizational learning aspects must be considered and the events must reflect the latest theoretical, in particular pedagogical, considerations as well as all sorts of contextual circumstances. It is suggested that the World Bank reengineer its institutional capacities as well as its current learning

---

35. Instead of using the term *learning event,* the World Bank often uses the term *training.* This term is defined as a means of supporting persons, mainly governmental officials, to affect their workplace behavior for the purposes of supporting the achievement of broader development objectives (IEG 2008a). According to another more detailed definition, training typically lasts a few days, and training programs are intended to raise awareness, build capabilities, build team effectiveness, or develop leaders (Goldstein and Ford 2002).

concepts to deliver such elaborate learning activities (see subsection 4.3.2).[36]

The pressure to achieve these goals is high. The latest world development indicators conclude that today there are more poor people and that poverty reaches further into middle-income countries than ever before (World Bank 2008). With the acceptance of the MDGs, the international community showed its dedication to cutting worldwide poverty in half by 2015 (UN 2000a, 2000b). Adequate capacity development is considered one of the critical missing factors in current efforts to meet the MDGs to reduce poverty, accelerate economic growth, and improve sustainable development (IEG 2008d).

In 2008, among other international organizations, the World Bank reiterated its focus on learning by renewing its knowledge and learning initiative and naming it as one of its six strategic directions (World Bank 2008). It decided to increase its efforts to find better and more efficient ways to improve its overall learning programs. As evaluation results have shown, based on contemporary theories and past experiences, and considering contextual circumstances of governments, there is much potential to improve the quality of governmental learning events.

2.3 Particularities and Lessons

A closer look at the experiences of learning in governments seen both from a historical perspective and from a current perspective allow the derivation of a full range of particularities, characteristics, and learning barriers that need to be taken into account in the development of a new concept of governmental learning.

2.3.1 Particularities and Barriers

The practice of governmental learning is a complex and hard-to-conceptualize matter. It must address numerous characteristics that appear to be found only in governments among policy actors, governmental institutions, and the political frame of action. Learning in governments has to take into consideration all sorts of cultural, economic, political,

---

36. The evaluation report, which reviewed the World Bank's main learning unit, the World Bank Institute, concludes that if the institute is to play a capacity-building role, its training processes need to be "substantially reengineered" (IEG 2008a).

psychological, religious, and social particularities and barriers, as well as other practical constraints that might hinder or even prevent learning at all (Tuchman 1985; Simon 1997; Chapman 2002; Kemp and Weehuizen 2005).

A closer look at these typical government phenomena reveals a distinctive set of dimensions that do not exist for individuals or single organizations as learners. Although governments consist of people and institutions, their learning behaviors are different from individuals and organizations. State officials, politicians, and civil society representatives—as well as their institutional bodies—learn in particular environments, which follow their own sets of logic, rules, and patterns. The specific knowledge that governments are supposed to learn is likewise different from what an individual or a private organization is used to learning.

The first set of particular characteristics of government learning focuses on the institutional aspects of a government:

1. Governments cannot be reduced to one organizational unit. They are composed of a distinctive set of institutions, including the ministerial cabinet, the parliaments, the courts, and the civil service. In regard to the governmental decision-making process, it makes further sense to consider other external civil society and private sector organizations as part of an extended understanding of what governance is. According to the principle of checks and balances, the different governmental and nongovernmental bodies do have different principles, tasks, and managerial responsibilities, which can be in opposition to each other in the process of developing and executing joint policy decisions.

2. In practice, governmental bodies have distinctive organizational cultures and agendas; some are hidden and hard to understand from the outside. This coexistence of different governmental institutions and nongovernmental organizations, each with various organizational styles and behaviors, makes them vulnerable to turf wars and internal queries. Governmental institutions are in constant risk of getting too preoccupied with internal conflict resolution and negotiation, making the end users' performance secondary to other considerations.

3. Governments act in a constitutional frame that is based on the principles, tasks, and responsibilities of democratic governance. With the development of democratic societies, these elements of a comprehensive governance agenda changed, adapted, and multiplied. It is therefore more likely that such principles collide with political constraints and result in poor or inadequate governmental behavior and decisions in day-to-day practice.

4. Unlike other types of organizations, governments do not have a definable audience whose expectations and needs have to be addressed in equal or at least comparable terms. Instead, they are obliged by their constitution to fulfill the needs of all citizens from all levels of society. This challenge is even harder in a globalized world, where constituents' assumptions are becoming more elusive and diverse than ever before.

5. Governments are traditionally responsible for the delivery of a wide range of public services and public goods that affect almost every vital aspect of their constituents' lives. Many of these goods and services are produced and delivered by the government itself, or under its supervision. Governments therefore hold in many areas a monopoly position with no or limited competition.[37] To maintain the quality of their deliveries, they are in the unique position of setting as well as verifying their own quality standards. The difficulty of this may be one reason why only a few governments have evaluation programs and why among these governments even fewer base their political decisions on evaluation findings.

6. Governing is about long- and short-term political activities. The former are about strategies to improve the quality of democratic governance. These are usually determined during the election process, where prospective governments persuade the citizens and/or electorates to vote for their political platform. The latter are rather ad hoc in nature and target instant political gains. In today's practice, they tend to dominate the day-to-day business, whereas the more reflective and

---

37. This may have changed some in recent years, where in the course of new public management concepts governments have devolved public tasks to the private sector or other forms of collaboration like public-private partnerships. However, even though governments are no longer the only actors that deliver public services and goods, they continue to hold the final political as well as legal responsibility.

learning-oriented long-term activities appear to lose weight in the governmental decision-making process.

A second set of characteristics is directed to the different policy actors in a government and their reasons for resisting or even blocking governmental learning:

1. Among the many reasons politicians are elected or reelected is their political program. Potential executives present their political goals and ambitions, which they intend to introduce after the election. Elected leaders in governments that are committed to their political promises tend to be hesitant to deviate from such programs, even when political circumstances and experiences indicate a reason to do so. There is some fear that changes from the policy platform after the election could be perceived as unfaithfulness to the constituents. In contrast, some politicians change their political positions opportunistically, depending on the results of public polls. This increasingly common behavior represents another strong barrier for learning.

2. Unlike other organizations, governments—or the elected actors—usually have fixed terms.[38] As a consequence, they have limited time to fulfill their political programs and promises as well as to deal with unexpected challenges. This puts politicians under pressure to decide which political issues they want to deal with first. The stress of this priority setting usually becomes more intense toward the end of a term, when reelections are impending.

3. Politicians define themselves through their exclusive and, in comparison to their competitors, superior expertise on specific political issues. They believe that, among other reasons, they get elected because of their unique political profile. In this light, politicians usually tend to be reluctant to participate in governmental learning events, where their participation alone could be misread as their admission of not knowing enough about a particular subject. There

---

38. There are also undetermined presidential systems, in which the head of state, usually a king or a queen, is appointed for life. However, these often-royal appointees tend to have limited and rather symbolic political power and are not further considered in the subsequent elaborations.

is a fear that opponents may use this to score points in the political process or in future elections.

4. Successful governmental learning induces behavioral change among policy actors. However, such changes by their nature have unpredictable risks. It is almost impossible to predict in advance which new behavior will end up being perceived as a win or a loss in the eyes of the target audience. For politicians it may therefore seem safer to keep the old behavioral patterns to avoid risks and potential mistakes, even though behavioral change may be the most promising and logical option in a given situation. A similar *no risk-taking* behavior is observable among civil servants, who traditionally have operated in an environment of secrecy and uniformity. Comportment that is considered new or different from mainstream behavior gets easily sanctioned and is therefore often eschewed among staff in public administrations.

5. Governments are composed of a multitude of personalities with various ambitions, experiences, and intellectual and physical capacities. Depending on the constellation of personalities and psychological dynamics in a group of policy actors, unforeseeable and unpredictable paternalistic coalitions may emerge. These can end up shaping the position of an entire government. As a consequence, pressing decisions or interventions will not be made, even though they are in line with former positions of the very same government.

6. The concept of the *iron law of oligarchy* states that all political leaders and other elites in governments, regardless of how democratic or autocratic they may be at the beginning or their career, are in danger of developing oligarchic behavior.[39] Over time the faction that has political power over others becomes a dangerous and unpredictable mean in itself, to which all other political rationales may get easily subordinated. The concept predicts that over time leaders seek power over others only to lose it over themselves—a mechanism that makes this undemocratic process even harder to control.

---

39. The rationale of the concept of the *iron law of oligarchy* lies in the technical indispensability of leadership, the tendency of the leaders to organize themselves and to consolidate their interests, the gratitude of the led toward the leaders, and the general immobility and passivity of the masses (Michels 1911).

As Karl Deutsch famously remarked, only those in power can afford not to learn (Deutsch 1963). It is therefore essential that individual and organizational particularities and barriers in governments, as elaborated above, be taken into account, in order to increase governmental learning. This does not diminish the widespread honest intents of governments and their respective policy actors to be eager to learn and to improve the quality of democratic governance. However, it would be imprudent to ignore the learning barriers in a given learning process that exist in the political reality of a government.

2.3.2 Lessons from Past and Current Practices

As presented in the analytical elaborations so far, substantive information does exist about how governments learned in the past and how they learn today. By reviewing this knowledge, a set of specific lessons can be derived that indicate what should be considered, emphasized, avoided, and so forth when developing a new concept of governmental learning.

1. Practice in governmental learning has shown that to date all three of the learning approaches contribute to the quality of democratic governance in their own way. However, each has its shortfalls, which have to be overcome to gain its full potential: If governments *learn by doing*, they should do so through a systematic review of their past performances to project appropriate future actions. If governments learn from others, the newly acquired knowledge should first be transformed into contextual political conditions before being applied. This step is even more advisable if the adopted new knowledge is based on so-called normative best practices. The transformation of knowledge into the situational context also leads to increasing ownership from a government for a particular political change. And last, if governments learn from each other, it makes sense if they do so in an ongoing, iterative process that reflects all different perspectives in regard to the knowledge to be learned.
2. The practical application of these learning approaches takes place in various types of organized events. To engage policy actors in learning activities requires an event design, in which the knowledge to be learned is based on the participants' experiences. In this understanding there is no distinction between speakers and audience. Every

participant or learning actor is considered a knowledge contributor and knowledge recipient alike.

3. To engage policy actors in such an interactive and participative learning process is not just the result of a natural course of action. The process has to be systematically initiated and structured to ensure that all perspectives reflecting the complexity of democratic governance are recognized and processed. The appropriate form of communication has to be based on dialogue. This signifies that specific communication rules have to be explained to participants and imposed by the event moderator.

4. Successful governmental learning requires individual as well as organizational learning considerations. The focus of this integrated learning is twofold: First, an appropriate learning design has to be applied to enhance behavioral change at the individual actor level; second, to enable policy actors to apply the newly acquired knowledge in their political environment, the directly affected governmental units have to be changed too so they support and reinforce the changes on the organizational level.

5. Governments are characterized by a number of particularities and learning barriers. Among these governmental challenges are activities such as settling conflicts between competing governmental units, harmonizing different organizational cultures, complying with a growing number of constitutional and democratic principles, coping with citizen expectations that cover almost every aspect of human life, dealing with limited private competition, and compromising between short-term politics and longer-term policy interests. Other noteworthy issues are the often-inflexible or opportunistic adherence of politicians to their political programs, their restricted leeway (because of fixed terms and term limits) in setting priorities, their eagerness or lack of it to take risks that may result from behavioral change, paternalistic alliances between policy actors, and the exposure of political elites to the abuse of political power.

All the lessons in this chapter have to be taken into account when developing a comprehensive concept for organizing governmental learning events. That concept must include a systematic review of past and current practices; the review has to be made from different perspectives; the resulting insights have to be adapted to the particular context in which they will be applied; the participating learning actors are knowledge contributors and knowledge recipients alike; and the way they interact with each other follows the communication rules of dialogue. And last, the concept has to target behavioral change not only on the individual but also on the organizational level, and it has to consider any possible learning barriers that exist in today's governments.

3 Theoretical Concepts of Governmental Learning

The latest evaluation findings about capacity development in democratic governance have shown that a comprehensive concept of governmental learning has to be based on systematically applied theoretical foundations (IEG 2008a). These theoretical considerations must first address a theory-based definition of the major terms related to the concept developed here. The theory-led description of democratic government, democratic governance, and governmental learning will be made on the basis of system theory and policy analysis concepts (see section 3.1); the process by which knowledge in democratic governance is produced and described in regard to its consistency will be in accordance with the concept of the knowledge creation cycle (see section 3.2); and because governments are composed of individuals and their respective institutional environment, the contemporary individual and organizational learning theories will be reviewed in regard to their contribution to enhance behavioral change from policy actors and their governmental bodies (see section 3.3).

3.1 Democratic Government, Democratic Governance, and Governmental Learning

Governmental learning has a longstanding tradition of empirical practice (see section 2.1), and in the past decades, there has been a growing attention to defining and developing concepts of learning specific to governments—that is, in terms of democratic government and democratic governance. The concepts of democratic government and their institutional and political environments (learning actor), democratic governance (learning content), and the understanding of governmental learning (learning activity) will be therefore elaborated next. Most of these concepts have their roots in systems theory and political analysis. Consequently, a selection of these theories will be presented to the extent that they are relevant.

3.1.1 Concepts of Democratic Government and Democratic Governance

To develop a governmental learning concept it is essential to have a proximate understanding of how democratic governments are composed and to what extent they collaborate with other societal and political actors and networks that are involved or that have influence in the governmental decision-making process.

Contemporary political theory literature uses the term *democratic government* to refer to a complex set of formal institutions and actors representing the state that has the monopoly of legitimate power. A democratic government is characterized by its ability to make decisions and its capacity to enforce them in a legitimate institutional frame (Stoker 2000; Eggerston 1990). In this understanding, a democratic government embraces all elected and appointed policy actors or public officials, who represent the executive, legislative, and judicial bodies, as well as the civil service with its numerous internal departments and agencies and its state-owned and/or controlled enterprises.[1]

Besides these governmental institutions, there is a highly fragmented maze of nongovernmental organizations and private stakeholder groups that are directly or indirectly involved in the complex process of governmental decision making. They include the private sector—corporations, business associations, and lobbying organizations—and organizations such as political parties, civil society organizations, grass roots movements, think tanks, academic organizations, the media, and social networks. These last include virtual communities, which communicate through blogs, Facebook®, Twitter®, etc. and are becoming an important and hard-to-control force in the political decision-making process. And last, and particularly relevant in developing countries, are international development and donor organizations, which have an increasingly strong influence on the political processes in their partner and client countries.

These nongovernmental pressure and interest groups are organized in more or less autonomous but interrelated centers, which are loosely coupled among each other and the official government (Weick 1995).

---

1. These types of enterprises deliver public goods and public services on a contractual basis for governments. For a further elaboration on this topic, see the literature on New Public Management (Boston et al. 1996).

All these organizations together are commonly understood as a governmental system.

In practice, these nongovernmental organizations and private stakeholder groups do have various degrees of legitimacy and political and financial transparency. However, despite the involvement of multiple players in the governmental decision-making and implementation process and regardless the level of legitimacy of the involved organizations, it is solely the official government that bears the full legal, political, and to some extent moral responsibility for the final decisions made.

Considering the complexity of decisions in a globalized world (see subsection 2.1.1), democratic governments do have an increasing interest in relying on the experiences and opinions of nongovernmental organizations and private stakeholder groups (Rose 1993). The purpose of this reliance is twofold: first, governments expect to improve the quality of their decisions, and second, they hope that the involved organizations will support the implementation of the decisions made.

However, it is a particular characteristic of these organizations that they tend to be highly unpredictable because of their vulnerability to changes in their respective political and social environment. Changes at either the local and/or the global level—as well as technological innovations—can easily shift political positions, which usually results in a redefinition of their political positions and strategies. This in turn affects their relationship with and influence on the official government and the respective governmental decision-making process (Kooiman and Van Vliet 1993). Furthermore, what makes these organizations and groups even harder to deal with is that their intentions and interests are often hidden or opaque, which further increases their unpredictability and unreliability.

The conglomerate of governmental and nongovernmental organizations and private interest groups and their representatives who debate, negotiate, and mediate with each other over political decisions and their implementation—as well as the entire process—are commonly called *democratic governance* (Doornbos 2003). This term refers to a complex multiorganizational structure of institutions and stakeholders that are drawn from government and beyond. Democratic governance is therefore what government does in collaboration with a more or less targeted selection of other societal actors.

Today there exist a broad range of theoretical definitions of democratic governance.² Many are based on historical derivations of how governments and their democratic agendas evolved over time (see subsection 2.1.1). Most of the contemporary understandings, however, overlap in many aspects and can be grouped around the three following domains of policy, politics, and polity (Pleasant Breeden 1972):

1. A *policy* is a deliberate collective agreement about substantive principles according to which decisions are made. In a democratic system, these principles relate to the distribution of power among institutions of government; the legitimacy and authority of state institutions; rules and norms that determine who holds power and how decisions are made about the exercise of authority; relationships of accountability among state officials and between these officials and citizens; and the impact of institutions and policies on public welfare and human rights.
2. *Politics* represent the democratic processes by which decisions are made. These decision-making procedures focus on the tasks of a government to determine which and how public goods and public services have to be delivered to best match citizens' preferences and needs.
3. A *polity* refers to a government's organization and its institutional and administrative bodies, which fulfill its responsibilities of delivering public services and public goods. This includes in particular the management of the administrative and fiscal affairs of the state.

In summary, democratic governments are the legally and politically responsible final decision-making and implementation bodies that are composed of the executive, legislative, and judicial bodies as well as a multitude of civil service departments, agencies, and state-controlled enterprises. Democratic governance in its own right refers to the collectivity of governmental and other nongovernmental and private stakeholder organizations as well as social networks and international donor and development institutions that are openly or covertly involved in the governmental decision and implementation process. These decisions are

---

2. For further definitions see Punyaratabandhu 2004; Doornbos 2007; Graham et al. 2003; Stoker 2000; and Cutting and Kouzmin 1999.

about the implementation of democratic principles (policy), delivery of governmental task (politics), and managing appropriate governmental institutions (polity).

3.1.2 Policy Analysis and Governmental Learning

As complex as the definitions of democratic government and democratic governance appear to be, the different policy analysis concepts that try to capture the complexity of learning processes and structures in governments are just as broad and numerous (Sabatier and Jenkins-Smith 1993). One major and often-referred-to concept derives from the classical systems theory, as interpreted and introduced in the policy analysis discipline by David Easton (1965a).

The fundamental argument of systems theories is based on the assumption that governance can be conceptualized as a system of input, throughput/withinput, and output (see Figure 1[3]). The inputs are demands from groups and individuals for political or policy initiatives, as well as pressure from the population and interest groups in general. The outputs are policies with a feedback loop, reflecting responses to the policies that initiate another round of political demands. In this model, governments are the linking element (throughput/withinput) that transforms demands of the public (input) into the policies enacted (output). This concept's comparative advantage is its high level of generality and applicability to political systems—from tribal governments to the most advanced democratic political systems (Finkle and Gable 1971).

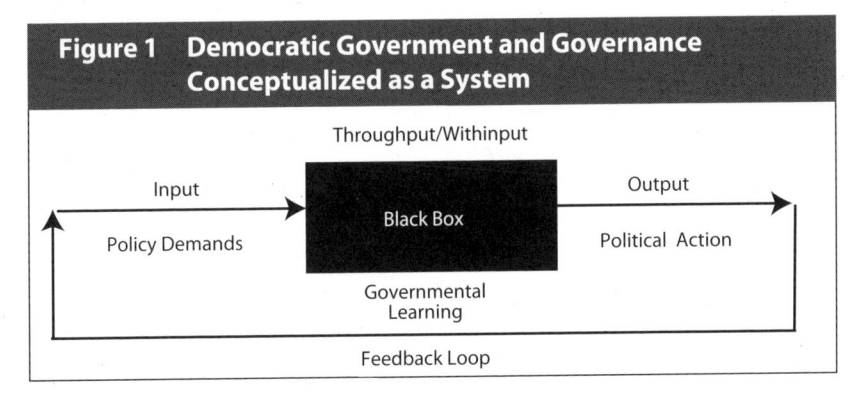

Figure 1 Democratic Government and Governance Conceptualized as a System

```
                    Throughput/Withinput
                    ┌──────────────┐
          Input     │              │     Output
        ──────────▶ │  Black Box   │ ──────────▶
        Policy Demands              Political Action
                    │              │
                    └──────────────┘
                    Governmental
                      Learning
                    Feedback Loop
```

---

3. This figure is very closely related to David Easton's systems analysis of political life model (1965b).

Although intensively observed and analyzed, it is still unclear how this governmental transformation process takes place in detail. Major issues such as what incentives and motivations political actors have to respond to outside pressures and requirements, or what institutional conditions will allow them to act accordingly, are still far from fully understood. David Easton (1965b) calls the lack of clarity in regard to this transaction process the *governmental black box* (see Figure 1). The search to light the darkness of this black box of policy dynamics and to characterize its actors, processes, and resulting changes in ideas has been one of the main contributions of policy analysis theories (Grin and Loeber 2007). From a systems theory perspective, the particular focus of this book is therefore the *machinery* of governing in the black box, more than it is the relationship between the inputs of societal actors and the resulting policy outputs.[4]

However, even with a particular focus on the throughput, it is important to keep in mind that in governing, which implies making and implementing decisions, as well as staying in power, governments in democratic systems depend to a high degree on their social and political environment (Deutsch 1963). It is therefore critical for them to adapt and shape their internal processes and institutional prerequisites according to the ongoing societal and political changes. To leverage their capacities in doing this, governments are expected to understand societal dynamics and developments. They have to learn how to cope with complex political realities and to adapt their political behavior according to the new challenges.

To do this, governments depend on an efficient and accurate knowledge transfer (Grin and Loeber 2007), not only from within but also from outside of the governmental system. Knowledge has to be transferred among the policy actors in a government and between governments as well as with experts and stakeholders, such as members of parliament and representatives from civil society, corporate businesses, universities, think tanks, etc. In light of a globalized and ever-changing world, this knowledge is constantly undergoing changes and renewals, which have to be continuously absorbed by the policy actors and their respective governmental organizations. These actors subsequently translate

---

4. This has been intensively studied and researched by Sabatier (1987) and others.

the knowledge into political action. To support this process it is essential that the institutional structures in a government are also regularly reviewed and if necessary adapted to new knowledge.

This focus on the learning of policy actors and related changes in government structures is called *governmental learning*.[5] By definition, governmental learning refers to a change in thinking—not just any change in thinking, but a structured, conscious change about a specific policy issue. This change in thinking does not necessarily result in instant and evident behavioral and/or institutional change. However, it is expected that in practice a well-designed learning process will gradually become real and visible through behavioral and structural change and finally emerge into concrete and adequate policy action (Kemp and Weehuizen 2005). The fact that governmental learning in specialized events will work out that way implies a well-designed and elaborate learning process.

3.2 Knowledge in Democratic Governance

Governmental learning is above all about knowledge in democratic governance and its transfer among the different actors within and outside governments (Kemp and Weehuizen 2005).[6] However, knowledge in democratic governance in a globalized world is in itself highly volatile and continuously changing (see chapter 2). This difficulty in conceptualizing the understanding of knowledge in democratic governance complicates learning for governments. It no longer seems clear how appropriate knowledge gets created, which internal and external instances are qualified to be involved in the creation and dissemination process, and to what extent the newly acquired knowledge stays

---

5. The term *governmental learning* as described here was initially introduced in the political analysis literature by Lloyd Etheredge (1981) and later integrated into a full-fledged theory of policy learning by Bennett and Howlett (1992). This latter theory includes three additional learning concepts—social learning, instrumental learning, and political learning—which together, and in contrast to governmental learning, emphasize input as well as output-related dynamics in a learning system (see also Connor and Dovers 2004; May 1992).
6. The term *transfer of knowledge in democratic governance* is used synonymously with *policy transfer,* which is defined in the literature as a process in which knowledge about policies, administrative arrangements, and institutions, etc. in one time and/or place is used in the development of policies, administrative arrangements, and institutions in other time and/or place (see Dolowitz and Marsh 2000).

relevant for governments over time. Such fundamental questions will be discussed in the following section, as their clarification is important.

3.2.1 Concepts of Knowledge Creation

The literature describes a variety of ways that knowledge is produced. Many of the models are based on elaborate knowledge creation cycles through which information gets transformed into knowledge and may later influence thinking and induce learning—and thus behavioral change.[7] Knowledge in this context is processed information whose meaning is attached to information by being connected to existing (processed) information. It is therefore knowledge—and not information alone—that provides insights for decision making (Davenport et al. 2008).

Knowledge can be tacit or explicit.[8] Tacit knowledge is semiconscious and unconscious knowledge held in peoples' heads and includes feelings and emotions. It tends to be what is understood without being openly expressed. In contrast, explicit knowledge is structured and accessible to people other than the individuals originating it. Explicit knowledge can be expressed in written or verbal terms (Nonaka and Konno 1998; Leonard and Sensiper 1998).

Our model defines knowledge creation as the result of gathering information (collection), converting it into a theoretical framework (configuration), and making that framework available to the public (dissemination) with the expectation that it will be applicable and usable in practice (application) (see Figure 2).[9] This cycle of creating knowledge, a so-called *ideal type model*,[10] distinguishes between the perception of

---

7. For an overview of the discussion of different meanings of knowledge cycles see Cowan et al. 2000; Edwards 2000; Fleck 1997; Schoen and Rein 1994; and Nonaka 1991.
8. The two terms were originally introduced by Polanyi (1967) and further developed by numerous authors like Nonaka and Konno (1998), Hildreth and Kimble (2002), and Leonard and Sensiper (1998).
9. This approach is closely adopted from the knowledge management used in the World Bank's documents, with a somewhat different terminology (see IEG 2003). For another similar model for knowledge creation seed the one of the Intergovernmental Solutions Program at the Center for Technology in Government, University of Albany, State University of New York (see www.albany.edu/igsp/practice/igknowledge.htm).
10. This term by Max Weber (1921) describes an analytical tool that is designed to simplify and explain complex cohesions. The drawback of the use of these *ideal type*

Figure 2 The Knowledge Creation Cycle

Knowledge Dissemination

Social Reality
Knowledge Application

Single Turn

Abstract Reality
Knowledge Configuration

Information Collection

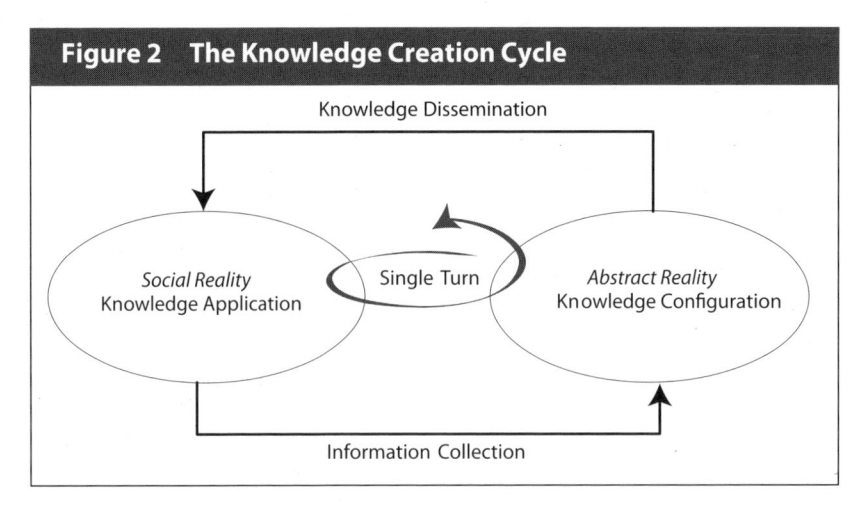

knowledge in a social reality and in an abstract reality. The former can be equated with the complex reality of everyday life, which individuals experience in real time. The latter is a somehow distanced abstraction of this social reality. It becomes real through the systematic observation, compilation, and categorization of everyday life processes.

The knowledge cycle is launched when an independent observer with a particular interest in a chosen area of social reality deliberately observes activities and occurrences. The observations collected are information, with no further given context or explanation. To be understood and have meaning, and to allow theoretical concepts to be derived from it, the information has to be thoroughly analyzed and configured. This analytical work has to be done in an abstract reality, for example, in a scholarly institution, which allows the observer, who is becoming the knowledge holder, to make neutral and impartial judgments. Thus, the original information gets transformed into explicit knowledge, which subsequently is disseminated through verbal replies, publications, visualizations, and so forth. The designated recipients of the developed knowledge are the observed subjects themselves, as well as other individuals or groups that may have a particular interest in learning and applying the newly gained knowledge.[11]

---

models is that they are never perfect and they always do have their blind spots when explaining social reality.

11. This theoretical description of different roles in the knowledge production cycle is also reflected in the practice of governmental learning, as described in subsection 2.2.2.

This *single-turn* cycle is functional under the condition that the knowledge at hand does have a kind of *ideal type* consistency or fabric. It consists of four basic dimensions (see Table 2): (1) the complexity of knowledge that represents the number of different perspectives toward a specific content; (2) the quantity of knowledge, which reflects the content volume of a particular set of knowledge; (3) the range of knowledge, which describes the spatial and contextual relevance of the content; and (4) the turnover of knowledge, which measures the unit of time until the content loses its validity in a given space and therefore has to be changed.

Table 2 Knowledge Fabric

First Dimension: Complexity (Perspectives)	Second Dimension: Quantity (Volume)	Third Dimension: Range (Context)	Fourth Dimension: Turnover (Change)
Low	Small	Universal	Slow

This ideal type model of a knowledge cycle helps in understanding the process of knowledge creation in a real-world environment. It illustrates an abstract reduction of the complex processes of knowledge creation and therefore does not fully reflect the real-time and tacit processes of social reality. However, this theoretical abstraction is based on a concrete assumption of how knowledge is composed and therefore needs to be laid open to make the model traceable and verifiable (Weber 1921).

This ideal type of model for creating knowledge is based on the assumption that the complexity of the knowledge at stake is *low* and that there is only one major perspective possible in regard to its content. This viewpoint is very much based on the presumption that there exists a normative set of knowledge that is broadly recognized as the universally valid one (first dimension). The volume of such knowledge is generally perceived as *small*, clear cut, and rather easy to oversee and be understood (second dimension). It is in the nature of normative knowledge that its range tends to be *universal* and easily applicable any time and place (third dimension). And last, its lifetime tends to be long and its loss of validity and significance rather *slow* (fourth dimension; see Table 2).

Table 3 Knowledge Fabric in Democratic Governance

First Dimension: Complexity (Perspectives)	Second Dimension: Quantity (Volume)	Third Dimension: Range (Context)	Fourth Dimension: Turnover (Change)
High	High	Situational	Fast

In such an analysis of knowledge, the design of the knowledge cycle is understood as a one-time event (see Figure 2). Normative knowledge is perceived as long lasting, and only drastic circumstances, in which knowledge is repeatedly proven wrong, will be reviewed and eventually replaced, as the result of a new turn of the knowledge cycle. Knowledge creation is therefore a *stop-and-go* process, where it is unclear from the beginning when it will end and when it will resume (Willke 1997).

3.2.2 Knowledge Creation in Democratic Governance

The principles, tasks, and responsibilities of democratic governance emerged over time and became operational in developed countries over the last two centuries—and since the middle of the last century in developing countries. This process is far from being completed and because of ongoing changes in a globalized world, probably never will be. This democratization process was paralleled by ongoing changes and growing expectations of citizen preferences for public services and public goods, which are becoming increasingly expensive and complicated to deliver (see chapter 2).

As previously described, the understanding of today's complex democratic governance agenda can be categorized into three major expectations (see subsections 2.1.1 and 3.1.1): (1) to adopt and follow a comprehensive range of democratic principles (policy), (2) to determine and deliver a set of public services and public goods to satisfy their constituency (politics), and (3) to shape and manage the appropriate governmental institutions to deliver those goods and services (polity). To understand the consistency as well as the process of its creation, knowledge in democratic governance can be described within the framework of the following four dimensions (see Table 3):

1. Democratic governance depends to a high degree on citizens' preferences, which are shaped by cultural, economic, historical, and religious backgrounds. As a consequence, in regard to almost any policy issue, there are multiple tacit and explicit viewpoints that need to be taken into account to make sound and citizen-oriented decisions. Knowledge in democratic governance is therefore very complex, and governments are expected to consider a *high* number of different and often contradicting perspectives in their respective decision-making process.

2. In a globalized world, knowledge about numerous policy issues such as environment, health, transportation, etc. is developed and spread all over the world. To deliver state-of-the-art knowledge to the public, governments are under pressure to incorporate a *high* volume of new information and knowledge in their policy decision-making processes.

3. Individual and local circumstances and preferences have to be taken into account in the governmental decision-making process. Thus, contextual and *situational* criteria in policy making are becoming more important, whereas normative and universal approaches, which are relevant in a larger scope, are losing reach and relevance in democratic governance settings.

4. Thanks to today's elaborate information technology, citizens are better informed than ever about research and achievements in issues relevant to policy. Governments therefore are being pressured to acquire and integrate the latest know-how into their policy-making process. To meet citizens' expectations, governments conduct an ongoing process of replacing and changing existing knowledge with the latest available knowledge, which results in a *fast* turnover of knowledge in democratic governance.

As Tables 2 and 3 show, knowledge in democratic governance and the ideal type of knowledge feature opposites on any of the four dimensions. However, because the functionality of the knowledge cycle is based on the consistency of the ideal type of knowledge, it might not be applicable for knowledge in democratic governance. There is a legitimate concern that the elaborate knowledge cycle, with its systematic process of information collection, transformation, and dissemination (see subsection 3.2.1), is too time consuming and in many ways nonfunctional to deliver high-quality and policy-relevant knowledge in democratic governance.[12]

Among the deficiencies is the fact that the ideal type knowledge cycle focuses on the collection of universal information without attaching any situative meaning to it. However, the creation of knowledge in democratic governance requires the consideration of as much explicit and tacit knowledge related to a specific issue as is possible. As a consequence, all potential perspectives represented through the respective knowledge holder have to be included in the knowledge collection process.

The broad inclusion of all viewpoints related to a select set of knowledge leads inevitably toward an elusive volume of both explicit and tacit knowledge that has to be considered in the knowledge creation process. It is difficult for a single or a group of knowledge holders to conceptualize and oversee such a high quantity of knowledge.

Knowledge in democratic governance is situational and cannot be generalized or devolved into other political circumstances. This implies that the created knowledge regarding a specific issue has value only for the particular situation, and the process of knowledge creation has to be repeated whenever the situation changes. Knowledge creation is therefore no longer a singular process, but rather a multi-turn process.

Last, the half-life of knowledge in democratic governance is comparatively short and stands in contrast with the rather long-lasting ideal type process of knowledge creation. There is concern that knowledge produced in this model is outdated and not applicable once it reaches the target audience and therefore ends up being inappropriate and unreliable for decision making in policy matters.

Considering these weaknesses, the ideal type model of knowledge creation has to be redesigned for democratic governance to deliver appropriate knowledge (see Figure 3). To become relevant, the process

---

12. This conclusion is based on Helmut Willke's understanding of the concept of the *knowledge society* (1997) originally introduced by Daniel Bell (1976).

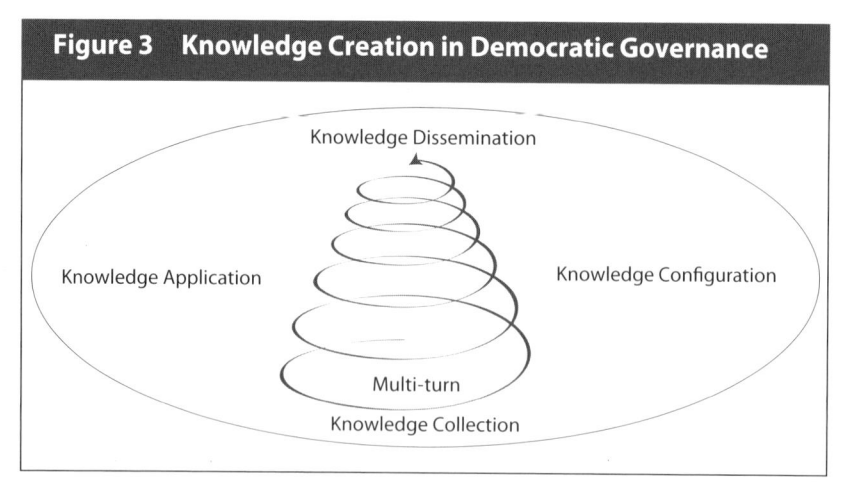

Figure 3 Knowledge Creation in Democratic Governance

- Knowledge Dissemination
- Knowledge Application
- Knowledge Configuration
- Multi-turn
- Knowledge Collection

of knowledge creation has to include all existing explicit and tacit perspectives regarding a specific policy issue, no matter how complex and voluminous the knowledge may be. The new model has to be responsive to situational circumstances, which may lead to frequent repetitions of the process; and finally, it has to take into account the short-term value of knowledge in democratic governance, which implies a considerable speed-up of the knowledge creation process.

This revised model of knowledge creation in democratic governance (see Figure 3) merges the original steps of knowledge collection, configuration, and dissemination into a simultaneous one-time exercise with no more distinction between social and abstract reality.[13] Knowledge production and its subsequent application become a real-time process, in which all individuals who represent a relevant perspective about a particular policy issue share their latest experiences. In such a process, there is no distinction between observed and observing subjects anymore. Everybody involved in the process is at the same time a knowledge holder and a knowledge recipient alike.

This kind of personalized knowledge is characterized by the meaning the knowledge holder gives it. It has therefore the same value as processed

---

13. This revised model of knowledge creation is inspired by an a World Bank initiative, in which the Poverty Reduction and Economical Development Sector, the Development Economics Unit, and the World Bank Institute launched a deliberate attempt to strengthen linkages across knowledge creation, sharing, and learning, and to connect directly to the knowledge needs of the Bank staff and client countries (see IEG 2003).

information. Because it is shared and expressed by individuals in a narrative and spontaneous manner, its articulation includes gestures and emotions and therefore reflects explicit as well as tacit knowledge aspects. Such knowledge represents probably the most accurate content in regard to a given subject in a given time and place. Once it is raised, it gets instant validation by the individuals engaged in the knowledge creation cycle. This has a positive effect on the quantity of knowledge, because irrelevant knowledge gets eliminated right away. Furthermore, the volume of knowledge will not become overwhelming in such an approach, because the individuals involved are their own masters and therefore will not voluntarily take on more knowledge than they can handle.

This kind of developed knowledge is also considered the most accurate and policy-relevant know-how. It is important to keep in mind that its reach is situational and applicable only in a given context. What may be the state-of-the-art knowledge in one political setting may be inaccurate or even counterproductive in another. Furthermore, the half-life of the knowledge at stake can be very short and needs to be replaced, depending on the political, social, and technical changes in a governmental environment. Because such changes are becoming routine, it is safe to say that this cycle of knowledge production is an ongoing iterative process. Whenever new democratic governance knowledge appears to lose its relevance because of new political circumstances or new priority setting, the process of knowledge creation or definition has to be relaunched. This fast and iterative process of knowledge creation is called a *multi-turn* process and is illustrated as a spiral in Figure 3.

3.3 Learning Theories

Governmental learning is about adequate and efficient knowledge transfer in democratic governance. In such a process, governmental representatives as well as other related knowledge holders play a crucial role in developing timely and meaningful knowledge. However, to what extent policy actors are willing and able to play their part in developing and subsequently applying new knowledge can be influenced by the pedagogical concept applied.

Furthermore, to apply the acquired knowledge in the political environment, appropriate institutional conditions are required to support the individual actors. In this understanding, not only individuals but also their institutional framework will have to change to learn. The concept presented here of how to organize learning events for governments is therefore not only built on individual but also on organizational learning theories, which will be presented in the subsequent chapters.[14]

3.3.1 Individual Learning

The following four individual learning theories represent the major contemporary pedagogical learning orientations (Tennant 1997). They are seen as discrete and competitive with each other. However, they all cover important perspectives of how learning at the individual level takes place.[15] The four theories are the Humanist Approach, the Cognitive Approach, the Social Approach, and the Behavioral Approach. These were mainly developed over the last two centuries and fit into a definite structure, as shown in Table 4.

The *Humanistic Approach* is derived from humanistic psychology (Maslow 1970; Rogers and Freiberg 1993; Watson 1913). In this approach, the basic concern is for the human potential for growth. Learning is seen as a form of self-actualization and self-fulfillment, which contributes to psychological health. Curiosity, personal freedom of choice, motivations, and feelings—as well as a sense of accomplishment and control of impulses—must be satisfied for such an *intrinsically motivated* learning process to take place. Finally, such a process is considerably enhanced if the individual feels a sense of comfort and physical security in his learning environment.

Learning in this approach is an informal and unstructured process that is motivated by internal stimuli (see Table 4). To get in a positive mood to learn, certain basic affective and emotional conditions must exist. To have his or her curiosity awakened, a potential learning actor needs to be aware that there exists a set of knowledge he or she does not know about yet. He or she has to develop a desire and an ambition to acquire that new knowledge—that is, he or she has to *want* to learn something. The attraction of entering into a learning process can be

---

14. Lloyd Etheredge (1981) deserves the credit; he was among the first authors to recognize the relation between the learning individual and the learning organization, which are all integrative parts of a learning government.
15. Regarding the rational how the four theories were selected, see Tennant (1997).

Table 4 Individual Learning Theories

	Internal Stimulus	External Stimulus
Informal, unstructured learning	**Humanist Approach** Learning through intrinsic motivation, comfort, curiosity, and so on.	**Social Approach** Learning through interaction, inspiration, transformaton, and so on.
Formalized, structured learning	**Cognitive Approach** Learning through discrepancies, discovery, differences, and so on.	**Behavioral Approach** Learning through extrinsic motivation, positive incentives, and so on.

increased when the new knowledge is presented from different angles, so the learning actor has the freedom to choose one perspective that relates best to his or her real-life situation. To increase the learning actor's curiosity, he or she must feel comfortable and secure in engaging in such an informal and unstructured learning process.[16]

The second theory is the *Cognitive Approach*, derived from the *Gestalt* psychologists (Lewin 1935; Piaget 1926).[17] This orientation focuses on an individual's mental processes—in other words, the act of knowing. Learning happens through *discovery* and *differences*. It results from inferences and expectations and from making connections. Through arranging a learning space or situation in which *discrepancies* between already known and unknown knowledge get highlighted, learning actors acquire plans and strategies for how and what they want to learn (Hartley 1998).

Accordingly, learning is a formalized and structured process that is also motivated by internal stimuli (see Table 4). In the Cognitive Approach the learning actor has to go beyond an unspecified feeling that he or she wants to learn something, as described in the Humanist Approach. Instead, the learning actor needs to be consciously aware that the new knowledge exists and must see the importance of getting

---

16. Maslow (1970) defines five levels of basic needs that have to be considered when setting up an optimal learning environment. These needs include physiological needs, safety needs, needs of affection and belongingness, needs for esteem, and needs for self-actualization.

17. *Gestalt* means configuration or pattern in German.

to know it to be motivated to enter into a learning process. To expand his or her cognitive competencies, the learner must actively expose himself or herself to an arranged learning situation in which he or she can discover and experience the difference between the known and the unknown knowledge, as well as have an opportunity to overcome the knowledge gap in a deliberate manner. It is preferable that this assimilation process be supported and arranged by a moderator.

A third theory is the *Social Approach* to learning (Bandura 1977; Mead 1934; Dewey 1933). Social or situational learning posits that people learn from observing other people, which also allows learning about implicit or tacit knowledge. Observations give individuals the opportunity to see the consequences of others' behaviors. They can gain some idea or *inspiration* of what might flow from acting one way or another. In this peer-to-peer exchange, behavioral change results from the *interaction* among individuals in a specific social or situational context. In these social situations the learning actors get an opportunity to *transform* and incorporate their observations into their existing behavioral patterns (Lave and Wenger 1991).[18]

Learning is an informal and unstructured process that is motivated by external stimuli in the Social Approach (also called the Situational Approach (see Table 4). A learning situation is carried out most effectively in a social context. Through interactions, individuals are exposed to other perspectives. Through this exposure, they may discover potentially explicit but also tacit knowledge gaps. Furthermore, by actively debating with their peers, individuals get inspired by new ideas and sets of knowledge. They learn about advantages and disadvantages of certain behaviors and experiences and as a result make their own judgments and assessments about what knowledge they want to integrate into their own course of action or their own social reality.

The final and probably most controversial theory is the *Behavioral Approach* (Watson 1913; Pavlov 1927; Skinner 1973). This orientation is based on the belief that one's inner experiences cannot be properly studied, as they are not observable. Therefore, the focus of learning should be on observable behavior; any change in behavior manifests learning. The knowledge to be learned has to be explicit, and what one is learning

---

18. This approach is closely related to the widely used method of situated learning and is the theoretical basis of communities of practice (see Lave and Wenger 1991; see subsection 2.2.2).

is determined by the elements in the environment, not by the individual learner. By consciously applying an appropriate stimulus in the form of *incentives*, a desired and measurable response is expected.

What makes this approach very much disputed among pedagogues is the element of *extrinsic motivation*, or behavior activated through externally introduced incentives. There is serious concern that this learning approach is unsustainable and the evocation of behavioral change may get reversed over time. That is particularly so with negative incentives. Research has shown that negative incentives such as penalization lead to negative responses—in some cases even to learning resistance.

In the Behavioral Approach, learning is a formalized and structured learning process that is motivated by external stimuli (see Table 4). Despite broad criticism on the impact of the behavioral approach on an individual's motivation to learn, there is a widespread belief in the conditionality between stimuli and response. Accordingly, well-thought-through and targeted provisions of incentives enhance individuals' motivation to enter into and successfully take part in a learning process. These measures are preferably positive. To deliver the intended and measurable behavioral change, incentives have to be well defined and carefully orchestrated through a well-designed didactical process.

These four self-contained learning theories can be categorized from two perspectives. First, theories can be distinguished according to the kind of stimulus that engages an individual in a learning process (Ramsden 1992). There can be *internal* as well as *external* stimuli. The former looks to the personal aspect of learning, which is seen as something that a person does to understand the real world. It is basically an internal voice or curiosity that gets a person involved in a learning process. With external stimuli, learning is something coming from the outside that unintentionally happens to or is done to the individual by another person.

The second perspective differentiates between *informal* and *structured* learning, as well as between *formalized* and *structured* learning (Rogers 2003). Informal and unstructured learning is seen as an unlimited and ongoing process. It is concrete, immediate, and confined to a specific activity. In this kind of implicit learning, the learner may not be conscious of the learning process itself. In contrast, formalized and structured learning arises from the process of facilitating deliberate learning based on concrete didactics. It is overt learning—learning because the learner wants to gain some information or skill—rather than the accumulation of experience. In other words, the learning actor is conscious of learning.

By applying the two perspectives to the four learning approaches, a specific logical progression can be developed that organizes the theories in a comprehensive order (see Table 4).[19]

In summary, by viewing the originally contradicting and competing learning theories in a sequenced and logical order, a comprehensive set of measures to enhance learning can be developed. First, a safe and comfortable learning environment has to be established to give the learning actor the opportunity to experience new knowledge, which may awaken his or her curiosity and interest. Second, the learner's motivation has to be further enhanced by setting up a deliberate didactic process in which he or she becomes rationally aware of the difference between the known and the unknown knowledge, as well as the importance of overcoming this knowledge gap. Third, the learning should be done in a social context, where the learning actor is exposed to different peer perspectives. This way he or she gets an opportunity to choose from a variety of different explicit or tacit knowledge and to think about how it may best fit into his or her individual social reality. And fourth, if actors are exposed to positive incentives and rewards, their motivation to engage in a learning process increases and supports the intended learning outcomes—a change of thinking and an intended change of behavior.

3.3.2 Organizational Learning

Practices as well as new concepts of governance show that knowledge in democratic governance is developed and implemented by a wide range of different governmental and nongovernmental organizations. These include the executive, legislative, and judicial bodies, as well as a multitude of civil service departments, agencies, and state-controlled enterprises. In the broad understanding of governance, they also imply the collectivity of

---

19. For similar models, see also the Encyclopedia of Informal Education: http://www.infed.org/biblio/b-learn.htm. There are various other ways the theories may be organized. However, for the purpose of this book's argument, the unintended overlaps and blurs are acceptable.

civil service and private sector organizations as well as social networks and international donor and development institutions. According to the principle of checks and balances, the different organizations do have various tasks, responsibilities, and control functions, which compete with or are complementary to each other in the process of selecting, developing and implementing policy decisions. Depending on the political subject matter, they continuously enter into and change coalitions to reach their political goals. In abstract terms they are organized in more or less autonomous, loosely coupled centers with various degrees of legitimacy and political and financial transparency (see subsection 3.1.1).

An important characteristic of governmental learning is therefore that a multitude of different organizational bodies are involved at some level in a specific policy issue. There is not only interaction between individual frames of thinking in one particular institutional unit, but also interaction between collective frames of thinking of different units (Kemp and Weehuizen 2005). As a result, learning in government cannot be reduced to the accumulated learning of "any of its constituent parts" (Etheredge 1981). Instead, it is essential that the perspectives of all governmental and nongovernmental bodies affected by a particular political issue be fully integrated in the learning process, to ensure a comprehensive understanding of the expected change. To ensure that accurate knowledge about a particular governmental body is considered, it is important that the most knowledgeable individuals of each unit be identified and engaged in the learning process.

As noted earlier, there are multiple barriers and obstacles in governments that can prevent learning (see subsection 2.3.1). To build up a political force that is strong enough to overcome such hindrances and to trigger a particular political change, it is crucial that—in addition to the participants, whose selection is based on their institutional knowledge—key stakeholders who mirror the political landscape are involved in the governmental learning process as well. An important purpose for their engagement is to ensure that the knowledge being learned is reviewed on an ongoing basis in regard to its political feasibility. It is further expected that these stakeholders will actively engage in the political process of implementing the newly acquired knowledge. Thus, they can build a strong enough and persuasive political power structure that shapes public opinion and acceptance about the envisaged governmental change.[20]

Organizational theories have shown that, depending on the kind of issues or knowledge, learning requires different types of organizational—or in the case of governmental learning—multiorganizational changes and interventions. These theories distinguish between three principal forms of learning: *single-loop learning* or *adaptation learning*; *double-loop learning* or *change learning*; and *deutero learning* or *process learning* (Argyris and Schoen 1974; Argyris 1990):[21]

1. If the purpose of learning—either explicit or tacit knowledge—is to improve institutional capacity, then it is called *single-loop learning*. Single-loop learning occurs when the existing mental maps or theories in use by a particular organizational unit or group of units are challenged by a political problem that calls for behavioral adjustments or changes at the governmental level. This type of learning enables a government to solve a particular problem to better carry out its overall policies and objectives.

   Single-loop learning is usually the intervention when a critical mass of political stakeholders representing a powerful enough coalition of organizational units agrees on a mismatch between expectations and outcomes of governmental actions and consequently pressures the government as a whole to take appropriate action. The goal of this type of learning is to make governments introduce political changes that allow them to realign their political outcomes toward the original intended and announced prospects. By doing this they are not questioning the underlying causal mechanisms that precipitated the original problem. In this approach error detection is seen as a necessary precondition for *error correction* (Leeuw et al. 1994).

---

20. For further theoretical elaborations on the term *key stakeholders* see Matthew Andrews' description of institutional entrepreneurs in development (2008a, forthcoming).
21. Single-loop and double-loop learning as originally introduced by Chris Argyris and Donald Schoen focus on the individual learning actor in the organization (Argyris and Schoen 1974, 1978, 1996; Argyris 1982, 1990). Inspired by Peter Senge (1998), who first added the perspective of the organization as a learning subject itself, this approach combines the individual policy actors and the various institutional units in a government as one collective learning subject.

2. In contrast, *double-loop learning* takes place when the applied intervention appears to be insufficient to solve the particular political problem, and therefore attaining the overall governmental policies and objectives is at risk. In this case the core elements of the mental maps are challenged and may result in changes not only regarding the immediate problem but in the strategies and preferences of the affected organizational units as a whole. So the assumptions underlying the policies and goals of a government might be fundamentally questioned, leading to the adoption of new and innovative solutions.

   A double-loop learning environment encourages questioning assumptions and confronting the traditions in a government that are being advocated. In this learning approach the underlying assumptions, norms, and objectives that pertain to the problem would be open to confrontation. That can also be the case with regard to assumptions underlying the selected policy programs, instruments, or organizational structures aimed at solving the political problem (Leeuw et al. 1994).[22]

3. *Deutero learning* occurs when organizational units learn how to carry out single-loop and double-loop learning. The first two forms of learning will not occur if organizations are not aware that learning must happen. Awareness of ignorance motivates learning. This awareness makes a government as a whole recognize that learning needs to occur and that the appropriate environment and processes need to be created (Nevis et al. 1995). By reflecting how organizational communication and decision making are handled, it is possible to detect what prevents open dialogue and learning. This kind of learning about how an organization itself learns improves its learning mechanism by overcoming its learning barriers (Bateson et al. 1956).

   As elaborated before, there are multiple reasons that governments may resist learning and by doing so act against their interests. One major explanation for this paradoxical behavior is rooted in inadequate formal or informal organizational rules. The former are usually the result of rules that were introduced in the past but lost their purpose over time. The latter tend to occur when policy actors try to cope with organizational pathologies such as steady and unusual heavy stress, workload, and conflicts. In both cases these rules compete and often contradict those rules,

---

22. For a case study on organizational learning from evaluation, see Nashat (2008).

which are necessary to maintain or to improve the performance of a government. Deutero learning is directed to disclose these negative formal and informal mechanisms and subsequently to get rid of them or replace them with new rules, which in turn are expected to overcome the existing learning barriers and improve the governmental learning capacities.

Whereas individual learning theories concentrate on the process of how individuals are acquainted with new explicit or tacit knowledge and are motivated to enter into a learning process by following an appropriate didactical process in an adequate social environment, organizational learning theories concentrate on the issue of matching outcomes with organizational expectations. When there is a mismatch, the organization strives to realign outcomes. However, if there is a serious mismatch that cannot be resolved by single-loop learning intervention, the underlying causal mechanisms that precipitate the mismatch must be taken into account. With this double-loop learning approach, the underlying assumptions, norms, and objectives that pertain to the problem get questioned. And finally, if single-loop and double-loop learning initiatives fail, it may be appropriate to reflect on the learning process itself by detecting negative rules and communication habits, which undermine an open and learning-oriented dialogue.

Therefore, from an organizational theory perspective, the initiation of governmental learning requires first the analysis of the type of problem at stake and second, if necessary, the detection and elimination of the existing barriers that prevent or hinder an appropriate learning process. Once the appropriate kind and level of intervention is determined, the governmental as well as nongovernmental units that are directly affected by the envisaged learning process have to be identified. The relevant stakeholders of each unit need to be selected to make sure that the learning activity considers the different organizational perspectives as well as the existing governmental power structure. This strategic selection and representation of learning actors is important for the subsequent implementation of the envisaged policy changes. It is expected that these stakeholders will act as opinion leaders and support the information and persuasion process of individuals inside and outside of government who were not involved in the learning process. The overall goal is the support of existing change agents to help them ensure the implementation of the envisaged political measures, within the existing constitutional and legal framework.

4 A New Concept of Governmental Learning—The Learning Spiral

The term *Learning Spiral* refers to the revised model of knowledge creation in democratic governance. It describes the development and transformation of knowledge into political action in a real-time and multi-turn process (see subsection 3.2.2).[1] The concept of the Learning Spiral is part of a comprehensive learning system, the methodology and process of which will be defined and described in eight distinctive stages, as well as discussed in regard to its practice in governmental learning.

4.1 Learning System and Learning Process

A learning system includes all elements necessary to ensure successful learning. The specific elements of a learning system cover a wide range of steps. They begin with the diagnostics—what knowledge a target audience wants to learn—and end with the system's implementation. The learning process is the central part of the system. In the process, a group of learning actors absorbs and adopts the new knowledge so it will ultimately influence their thinking and change their behavior in an intended way. The process of the Learning Spiral is therefore directed to enhance the prospect that the knowledge to be learned will end up being applied in practice in a given governmental system.

---

1. In the early stages of concept development, the *Learning Spiral* was called the *Knowledge Spiral* (Abderhalden and Blindenbacher 2002; Blindenbacher and Watts 2003). With the further development of the concept and its focus on the learning aspect of the process, the term was transformed into Learning Spiral. However, both terms are distinctively defined as originally used by Ikujiro Nonaka and Konno (1998) and Osterloh and Wübker (2000); they use the term Knowledge Spiral in the narrow context of organizational learning and knowledge management.

4.1.1 Learning System

Analytical and theoretical concepts highlight different aspects that have direct or indirect impacts on learning in democratic governments. However, not much has been said yet about the systematic and chronological course of action in which the practice of learning in governments takes place. As previously discussed, models that consider such a comprehensive understanding of learning derive from systems theory (see subsection 3.1.2) and describe the full chain of activities related to governmental learning.

The learning system presented here is largely derived from existing models such as the World Bank Institute's Global Development Learning Network and was further developed for the particular purpose of the Learning Spiral. The model is described according to the three systems—theoretical elements of input, throughput, and output—and subdivided into a chain of action with five major steps (see Figure 4).

1. The *input* is made up of the assessment and diagnostics—what knowledge is needed and/or requested from the concerned target audience (first step). It is followed by the selection of the knowledge to be learned, and—if that knowledge does not already exist—its creation (second step). The last step is the dissemination and distribution of the knowledge to the respective target audience (third step).

2. The *throughput* represents the learning process in which a group of learning actors, who are chosen from the target audience according to a set of criteria, is expected to absorb and adopt the new knowledge, and if necessary to adapt it according to the group's specific circumstances and needs through intra- and interpersonal procedures (fourth step).

3. The *output* in a learning system consists of the implementation of the new knowledge into practice by the learning actors (fifth step). It is part of an implicit understanding of the learning system that the implementation step itself is subject to a rigorous evaluation, preferably by an independent body, which reviews the output, the outcome, and the impact of the entire chain of learning activities.

The input- and output-oriented steps are considered the rational and predictable measures in such a learning system. They include identifying

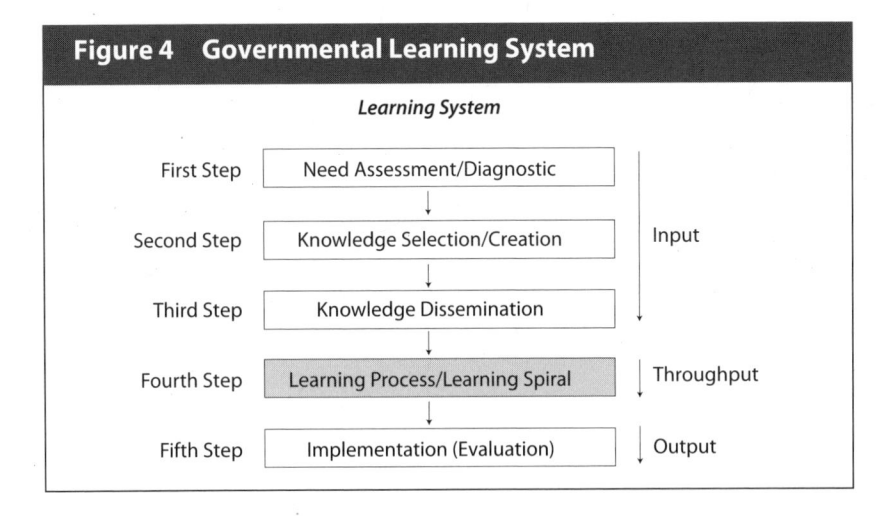

Figure 4 Governmental Learning System

Learning System

Step	Process	Stage
First Step	Need Assessment/Diagnostic	Input
Second Step	Knowledge Selection/Creation	Input
Third Step	Knowledge Dissemination	
Fourth Step	Learning Process/Learning Spiral	Throughput
Fifth Step	Implementation (Evaluation)	Output

the target audience and the knowledge it needs to learn, as well as its dissemination. The output includes the degree to which the new knowledge was implemented.

In contrast to these foreseeable and empirically comprising steps, the central element—the throughput—appears to be unpredictable and hard to conceptualize. What makes the learning process in particular difficult to control are the many particularities and learning barriers of governments (see subsection 2.3.1), as well as the complex and fast-changing knowledge in democratic governance (see 3.2.2).

To date, the learning process, which triggers the application of adequately diagnosed, defined, and disseminated knowledge in an intended manner, has not been sufficiently explored. In terms of the concept of policy analysis, this insufficiently explored area of the learning system is figuratively labeled according to the policy analysis concept as the black box of governmental learning (see subsection 3.1.2). The black box symbolizes the collectivity of human, organizational, political, and content-oriented factors that make the learning process in governments hard to predict and therefore difficult to manage.

4.1.2   The Learning Process and Its Methodology

The sharing of knowledge does not guarantee its adoption and application. Comprehensive learning in governments can therefore not be taken for granted (Rist 1994); it has to be actively and systematically pursued. Existing attempts to rationalize and structure learning processes through political conditionality alone appear to be insufficient to fully consider the complex dynamics of informal and political processes and focus primarily on the predictable and observable mechanisms of learning (see subsection 2.2.1).

The purpose of the concept of governmental learning developed here is twofold: to organize the learning process in order to address particularities and learning barriers that prevent governments from learning, and to consider the tacit and elusive characteristics of knowledge in democratic governance. Such an elaborate learning process is expected to enhance the implementation of newly learned knowledge by the chosen learning actors in their self-defined direction. In terms of a learning system, this learning concept fills the gap between the dissemination of knowledge and its implementation; by doing so, it sheds light on that black box of governmental learning (see Figures 1 and 4).

The fundamentals of the learning process were developed by following a *heuristic* procedure. In this context, heuristics stands for strategies using readily accessible, though loosely applicable, experiences and theories to control problem solving in human beings and machines.[2] Accordingly, the development of the Learning Spiral concept is the result of a multiyear process, during which experiences in organizing learning events were systematically reviewed and subsequently complemented and improved by related analytical and theoretical concepts.

The theoretical fundamentals of the learning concept go back to experiences with governmental learning events organized in the federal administration of Switzerland in the late 1980s, which where afterward further developed in bilateral and multinational learning events worldwide.[3] Common to all these early learning activities was the engagement of local and/or national governments, which were deter-

---

2. By definition, a *heuristic* is a method to help solve a problem, commonly an informal method. It is particularly used to come to a rapid solution that is reasonably close to the best possible answer, or optimal solution. Heuristics are rules of thumb, educated guesses, intuitive judgments, or simply common sense (see Michalewicz and Fogel 2000).
3. For an extensive description of the learning events held in Switzerland, see the book series published by the Swiss Federal Administration *(Schriftenreihe des Eidgenoessischen Personalamtes 1998–2001)*. For an illustrative example for an early multinational event, see the Second International Conference on Federalism 2002, which is described in detail in chapter 5.

mined to learn from their own and others experiences. Each event was carefully evaluated in regard to its quality as perceived by the participants as well as to its long-term impact on changes and improvements in the respective governmental settings (Blindenbacher et al. 2000). To improve these initial applications of the concept, the events were later reviewed and further complemented with new theoretical considerations and empirical evaluation. The revised concept was afterward reapplied in a new learning event and subsequently reevaluated and reviewed.[4]

Over the last decade the Learning Spiral has been applied in about 150 documented learning events. They occurred in all sizes and shapes, with thousands of participants from more than 100 countries, representing all levels of governments and nongovernmental organizations and held in more than 20 different countries.[5] The ongoing replication of this dialectical procedure of practical application on one side and analytical and theoretical review on the other allowed ongoing development and improvement of the learning concept.

The number of analytical and theoretical concepts considered in this long-lasting process represents a full range of different models, which are based on a multitude of different academic backgrounds as elaborated in chapters 2 and 3. Their compilation shows a kaleidoscope of theory-based disciplines (see Figure 5), which were used to describe and understand how governments learned in the past and how they learn today (see sections 2.1 and 2.2), what their particularities are, what lessons can be drawn (see section 2.3), what the existing governmental learning theories are (see section 3.2), what the knowledge is that governments are supposed to learn and how it gets created (see section 3.2), and, finally, what individual and organizational learning theories can contribute to improving the quality of governmental learning (see section 3.3).

---

4. This methodology is based on the scientific concept of "critical raationalism" developed by Karl Popper (1935).
5. For a description of some of these activities, see Blindenbacher and Watts (2003), Blindenbacher and Saunders (2005), Blindenbacher and Brook (2005), Baus et al. (2007), and Blindenbacher and Chattopadhyay (2007). The countries in which such learning events were organized include Argentina, Australia, Austria, Belgium, Brazil, Canada, China, Ethiopia, Germany, India, Malaysia, Mexico, Nigeria, Pakistan, the Philippines, the Russian Federation, Republic of Korea, South Africa, Spain, Switzerland, and the United States (in alphabetical order).

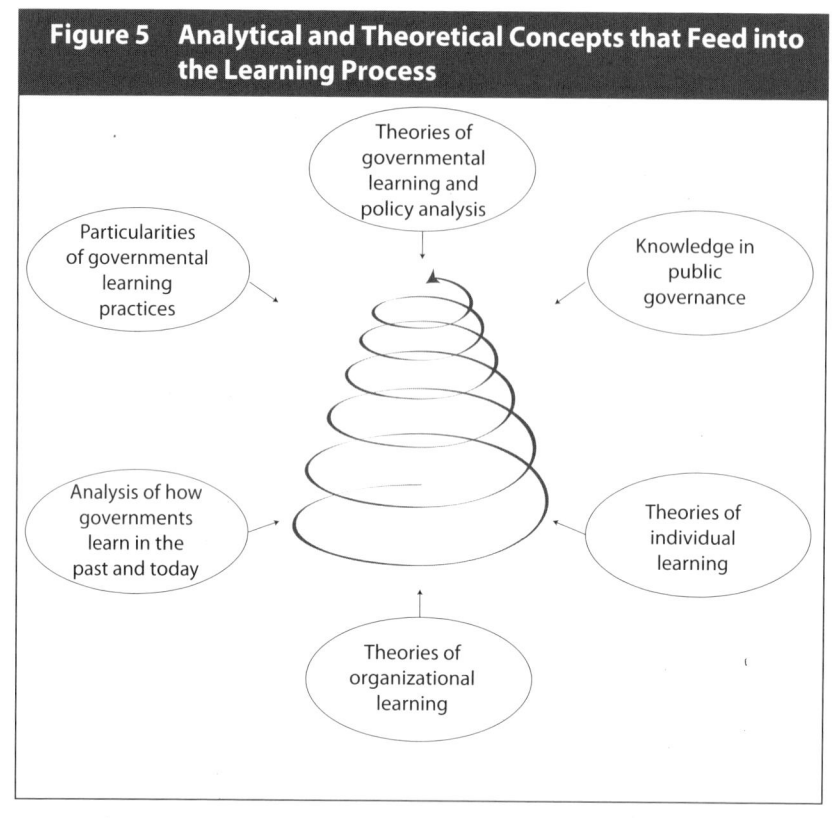

Figure 5 Analytical and Theoretical Concepts that Feed into the Learning Process

- Theories of governmental learning and policy analysis
- Particularities of governmental learning practices
- Knowledge in public governance
- Analysis of how governments learn in the past and today
- Theories of individual learning
- Theories of organizational learning

For the purpose of developing the Learning Spiral in a replicable template, the rationales of the different concepts were examined in regard to their contribution to the structure of this learning concept. This was done according to the methodology of the *qualitative content analysis*, which is a replicable and valid technique for making specific inferences from a given text—which in this case describes a set of theories—to develop a new theoretical concept such as the Learning Spiral.[6] Following this methodology, the deducted rationales were clustered around precisely defined subject matter and thematically organized around and sequenced into eight distinctive stages. Each stage was labeled with a self-descriptive term and described in such a manner that it serves as a practical and applica-

---

6. Per definition, the *quantitative content analysis* is a hermeneutic research technique for making inferences by systematically and objectively identifying specified characteristics from a text to other states or properties of its source (Krippendorff 1969).

ble guideline to organize any form or type of existing governmental learning events: Conceptualization, Triangulation, Accommodation, Internalization, Externalization, Reconceptualization, Transformation, and Configuration.[7]

4.2 Stages of the Learning Spiral

The following description of the eight stages of the Learning Spiral summarizes the most relevant subject matter derived from the analytical and theoretical concepts. For the purpose of traceability, each subject is codified with the subsection number(s) that indicate where it was referred to and explained. For ease in understanding, each stage is also graphically illustrated by a set of figures and summarized in functional terms that translate the abstract explanations into concrete measures, which must be considered when designing and carrying through a governmental learning event.

Stage 1: Conceptualization

The outset of the governmental learning process is a distinct collection of already existing knowledge on a particular issue in democratic governance that is relevant to a given government (subsections 2.1.1, 4.1.1). In the learning process, that knowledge has to be actively and systematically reshaped by an independent and nonpartisan event facilitator, who develops and implements an appropriate didactical design, which is based on the learning concept (subsection 2.2.2).[8]

Knowledge in democratic governance tends to be elusive and hard to oversee, so the knowledge to be learned has first to be framed precisely and explicitly (see Figure 6) (2.2.2, 3.2.2). If this is done, the complex content is made digestible so the target audience is not overwhelmed and as a consequence discouraged to enter into the learning process (3.3.1).

---

7. Most of these eight terms were developed according to the content they represent and as they are described in the forthcoming section. The exceptions to this pattern are the terms *triangulation, internalization,* and *externalization,* which already existed and which were further developed for our purpose to describe the Learning Spiral concept. The term *triangulation* was first introduced by Campbell and Fiske (1959) and the terms *internalization* and *externalization* by Nonaka and Konno (1998).

8. For the particular function of such a learning organization and its facilitator, see section 4.3.

To further stimulate the learning actors' intrinsic motivation and curiosity, the framed knowledge has to be described in a form that addresses the concrete political issues and problems of the expected participants (3.3.1). This should enable them to trust that the selected knowledge will improve their competence and abilities to better accomplish their political objectives (2.3.1, 2.3.2). The framed knowledge should also be presented such that it is relevant not only to the individual policy actors but also to their respective governmental and nongovernmental institutions (2.2.3, 3.3.2).

The half-life of knowledge in democratic governance is considered to be very short (2.1.1). To keep up with the ongoing changes of citizen preferences and technological innovations (3.2.2), the knowledge to be learned has to be constantly updated until it is reflected in the upcoming learning activity (2.2.1, 3.2.2).

In practical terms, the conceptualization stage includes all the planning and design of a particular governmental learning event as well as the framing of the given knowledge. This knowledge is based on the content that was determined by a proceeding diagnostic procedure, in which the needs of the target audience were identified. The selected knowledge has to be continuously transformed, updated, and complemented so it is made relevant for the potential learning actors and their respective governmental systems. The event facilitator oversees all these activities.

Stage 2: Triangulation

Today's knowledge in democratic governance is perceived as complex and difficult to predict (2.1.1, 3.1.1, 3.2.2). For any issue there are mul-

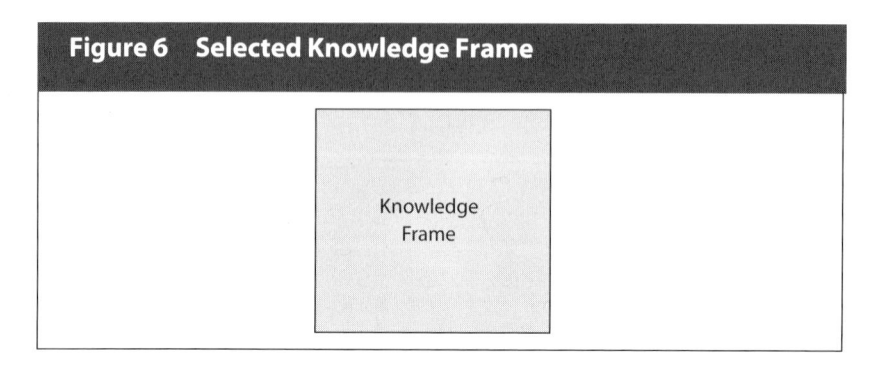

Figure 6   Selected Knowledge Frame

Knowledge Frame

tiple individual and organizational needs and expectations, all of which have to be taken into account to make citizen-oriented policies (2.3.1, 2.3.2). To get a comprehensive perception of the framed knowledge, all these situational perspectives have to be considered (content triangulation). This diversity of viewpoints allows a comprehensive and impartial understanding of the selected knowledge and increases its relevance for a wider audience (3.3.1). By providing different viewpoints in regard to the particular subject, the learning actors are recognizing new knowledge of which they may not have been aware before (3.3.1). To ensure that every relevant perspective is represented at the learning event, a primary stakeholder has to be chosen who is considered an authority in at least one of the selected viewpoints (2.2.2).

Because the implications of democratic governance affect a wide range of governmental and nongovernmental bodies, as many of these organizational units as possible have to be represented in the learning event by a primary stakeholder (stakeholder triangulation) (3.1.1, 3.2.2). These institutional stakeholders, together with the content representatives, are considered the core learning actors and need to be invited to the learning event (see Figure 7). The invitations are personal and cannot be passed on to other individuals (3.3.2). This broad selection of participants also ensures that the new knowledge has a higher degree of legitimacy and is less prone to abuse (2.3.1, 2.3.2).

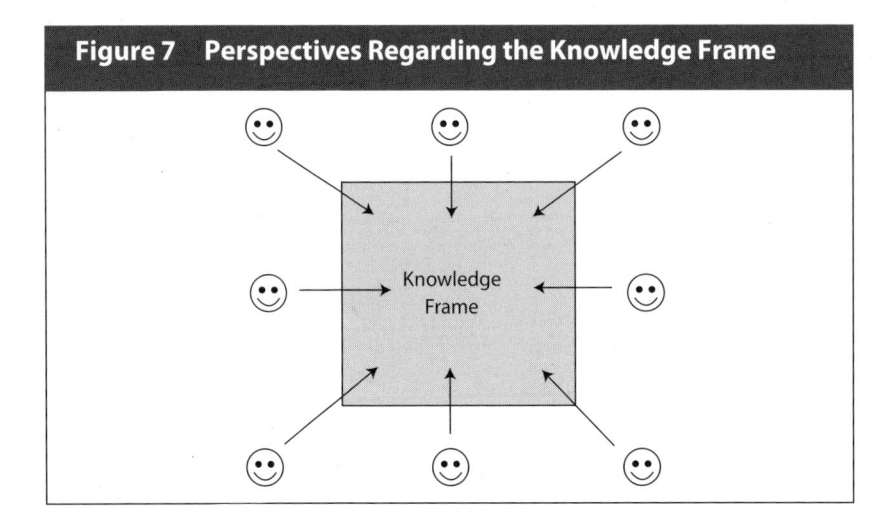

Figure 7   Perspectives Regarding the Knowledge Frame

The group dynamic concept of dialogue draws on the experiences of all participants involved the learning process with the aim of fostering a new collective understanding (2.2.1, 2.3.2). Every participant therefore has a role as both a knowledge holder and a knowledge recipient (2.2.2, 3.2.2). Participants are expected not only to know their particular perspective but to know what knowledge they are lacking and therefore looking for (2.3.2). It is expected that once a learning actor has confirmed his or her participation, he or she will be present for the complete learning process (2.3.1, 2.3.2).

In the triangulation stage, the selection and invitation of the learning actors is performed according to well-justified content and strategic criteria. These participants are chosen from among the originally defined target audience, which was involved in the diagnostic, selection, and dissemination steps of the learning system. The chosen learning actors are considered as primary stakeholders, who are invited on the basis of their personal and professional knowledge.

Stage 3: Accommodation

To set the stage a safe and inspiring learning situation must be created (see Figure 8) (3.3.1). The learning actors have to be fully aware of what their expected contributions and commitments are, as well as of what the potential risks and gains related to their engagement may be (2.3.1, 2.3.2). Thus, the learning process has to be transparent and actively communicated (2.2.1). This is done by the event facilitator, who oversees the event proceedings (2.2.2). This individual is also in charge of all organizational precautions (3.3.1).

Among the information to be communicated are the background materials and the procedures of the learning process itself (3.3.1). The former includes information about the learning activity operations and logistics. The latter addresses the content, the participants, and the event design. The learning actors must be aware that despite their different hierarchical positions, they are all treated equally (3.2.2, 3.3.1) and that they are all expected to follow the same communication rules (2.2.2, 3.3.2).

The way this information is communicated has to be sensitive to the cultural, economic, gender, religious, and social backgrounds of the learning actors (3.2.2). This information transfer has to be done early

Figure 8   Safeguarding the Knowledge Frame

[Knowledge Frame]

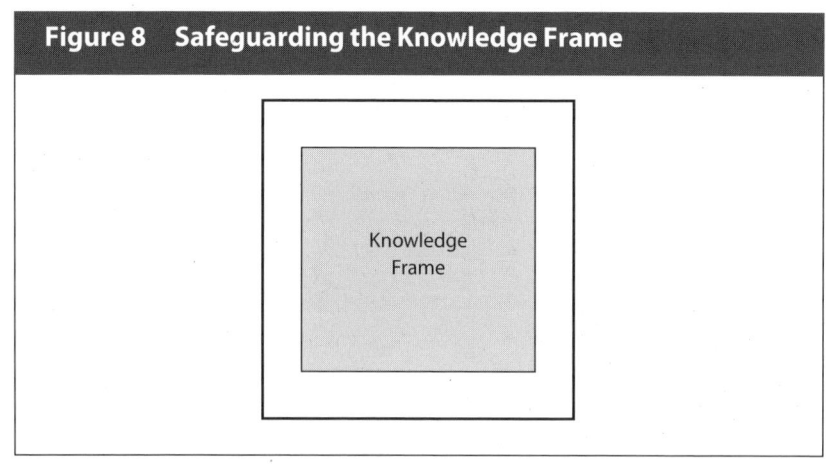

enough that changes in the agenda and/or other aspects of the learning procedures can be made whenever the circumstances require (2.2.2, 2.3.1). This early and continuous information policy helps build a sense of trust between the participants and the event facilitator as well as in the learning process, which itself helps to overcome potential learning barriers (2.3.1, 3.3.1).

In the accommodation stage, all practical and theoretical procedures have to be taken care of. That will ensure a learning environment that participants trust, as well as physical security and logistical comfort. The event facilitator has to set in place and communicate to the participants the event design, the agenda, the participant list, participants' functions, the communication rules, and so forth. This has to be done early, so that changes to these measures can be made whenever required. In this stage as well, all organizational tasks (lodging, transportation, food, and security) have to be planned. These activities need particular attention, because if not properly executed, they may have a negative impact on the participants' attitudes and engagement in the learning process.

Stage 4: Internalization

Once the basic organizational and emotional conditions in regard to the governmental learning process are in place, the selected learning actors are invited to get actively involved. In a first didactical step, they are expected to reflect on their own experiences in light of the original normative knowledge frame (3.3.1). This deductive and self-reflective approach opens the door for the individual participants to become aware of their current practices and to what extent those fit or do not fit into the given knowledge frame (see Figure 9) (3.3.1).

In this stage the participants are further expected to question the reasons that their previously made conclusions, such as the reasons their existing knowledge, match or do not match the given frame and whether this is a positive or a negative thing (3.3.2). This self-positioning enhances participants' consciousness of the differences between what they know and do not know. In this intrapersonal process, the participants' intrinsic motivation and curiosity to learn is enhanced in an intuitive manner (3.3.1).

In the internalization stage, the learning actors are brought together in a physical or virtual space. Here they have the opportunity to ask questions about the learning procedures and the knowledge to be learned. In this stage the event procedure has to provide a space that gives the participants time to think about overlaps and differences between their own practices and the presented knowledge frame. The participants are in particular expected to think about the quality of the differences and to what extent they have impact in the performance of their governmental system.

Stage 5: Externalization

In a second didactical step, the learning actors are invited to share their individual reflections with the other participants (see 3.3.1) (see Figure 10). In this interpersonal exchange they are expected to share not only

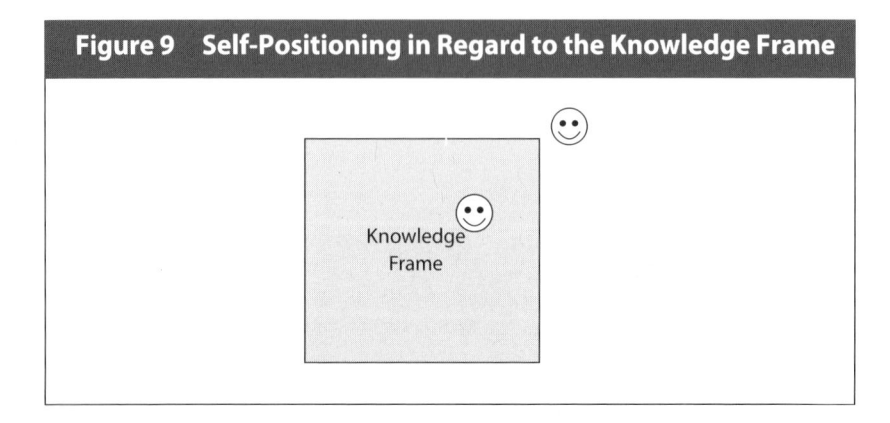

Figure 9   Self-Positioning in Regard to the Knowledge Frame

their successful but also their unsuccessful experiences (2.2.1, 2.3.2). This group interaction takes place through a dialogue (2.2.2). To ensure the quality of the dialogue, the event facilitator must enforce the communication rules and oversee the style of social interactions, to prevent the silent dispersal of negative communication routines that may disturb the process of learning (see 3.3.2).

In such an interactive setting, there are no prepared speeches or official statements. Participant contributions have to be short and narrative in style and are supposed to be spontaneous and reactive to the contributions made by others (2.2.1, 3.3.1). The given timeframe for statements does not allow participants to cover the whole subject. However, the time should be sufficient to describe a particular perspective (3.2.2). In this form of dialogue, tacit knowledge becomes explicit and therefore accessible to all participants (2.4.1, 3.2.2).

Thanks to the social group setting, the participants observe their peers when sharing personal reflections in a natural and unobtrusive way. This set-up motivates participants to follow that example (3.3.1). By giving voice to individual reflections, the learning actors get an opportunity to compare each other's experiences and to verify to what extent their reflections fit the given knowledge frame (2.1.2). This multidimensional comparison is intended to encourage participants to question the assumptions that underlie their present governmental policies and to

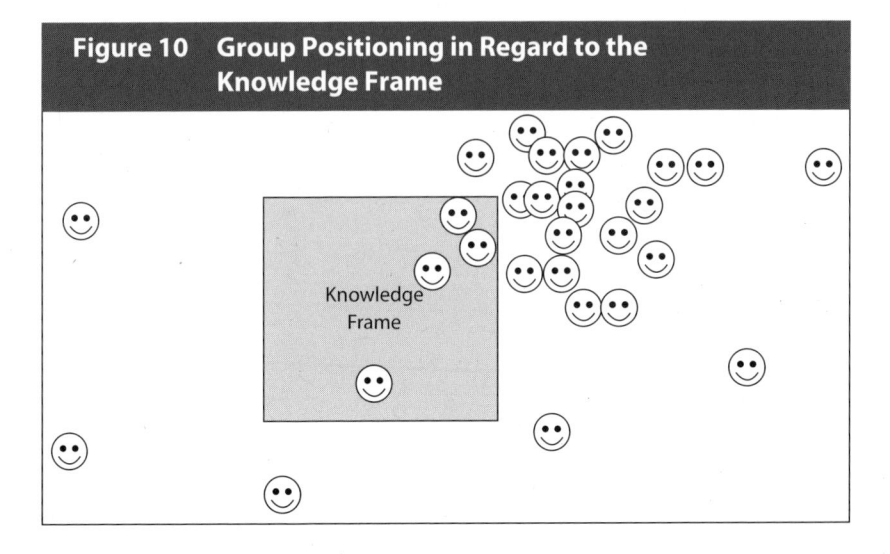

Figure 10 Group Positioning in Regard to the Knowledge Frame

challenge longstanding individual and institutional behaviors through creative and innovative ideas (3.3.2).

From the learning actors' point of view, this form of disclosing personal experiences to others is considered as the *admission price* to participate in the learning event. The *payback* for such an engagement is that all other participants do the same (2.2.2). By following this pattern, the learning actors are becoming knowledge holders and knowledge recipients alike, which in turn affords the unique opportunity to learn from each other's experiences in a transparent and interactive way (2.1.2, 2.2.2, 3.2.2).

In a structured dialogue participants are invited to share and compare reflections. They have to do this under equal conditions by following the communication rules, which the event facilitator enforces. In this second didactical step, the participants are in particular expected to think about the commonalities and disparities of the shared reflections as well as to what extent they overlap or differ from the given knowledge frame.

Stage 6: Reconceptualization

In the course of the first two didactical steps, the participants reflect, absorb, and share each other's experiences. In a third step the learning actors get an opportunity to exchange their opinions about possible compliances and differences between the presented reflections (2.2.2, 3.3.1).

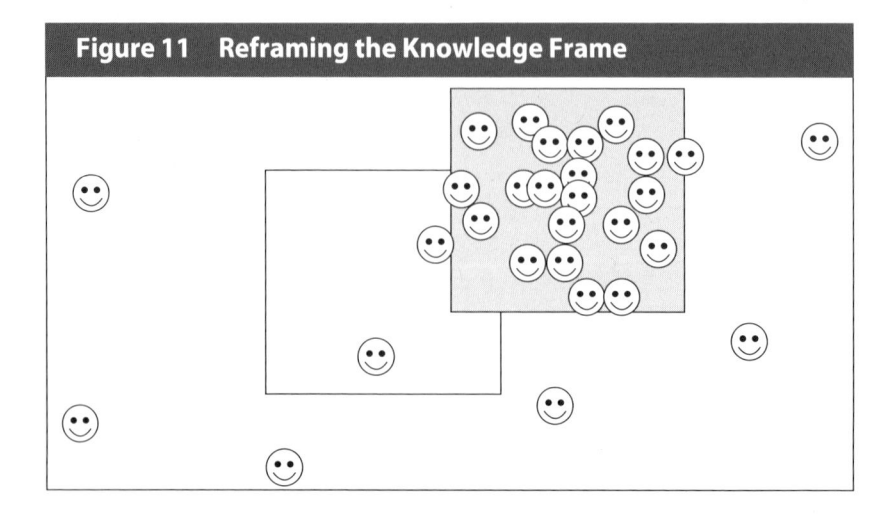

Figure 11 Reframing the Knowledge Frame

Depending on the thematic variance and distribution of shared experiences, a new cluster of overlapping reflections develops that gradually evolves into a new collective perception about trends and developments regarding the knowledge at stake (3.2.2). In this dialogue a new social reality is made explicit and transparent and therefore comprehensible and verifiable to every participant (3.2.1). The learning actors are now in a position to openly debate the new set of knowledge by comparing it with the original knowledge frame as well as to its practical relevance (3.2.1).

Following this real-time deductive procedure, a new normative frame of knowledge emerges to replace the original one (see Figure 11) (2.2.2, 2.3.2). This new frame is not necessarily based on a consensus among all participants, but it reflects a strong belief that this is the most relevant and up-to-date knowledge in dealing with the present problems and challenges in democratic governance (3.2.2).

The purpose of the reconceptualization stage is to review the existing knowledge frame and, if necessary, replace it with a new one. This reframing procedure is done in a dialogue, in which the learning actors search for a new set of knowledge that mirrors a majority of shared reflections. Through this process, the new collective understanding becomes visible and accessible to all participants. This new knowledge is considered the most updated and relevant for a majority of participants and therefore replaces the original frame of knowledge.

Stage 7: Transformation

Knowledge in democratic governance should match local expectations and circumstances (3.2.2). In a fourth didactical step, the newly developed, normative knowledge has to be deducted to fit the requirements of a given political reality (see Figure 12). For this purpose, the learning actors have to systematically assess the new knowledge in regard to their actual needs and create concrete plans and activities that may help improve the current governmental performance (3.3.1, 3.3.2). To further improve the quality of these so called *action plans*, the plans themselves are supposed to be shared and reviewed among all participants in a final dialogue (2.2.1).

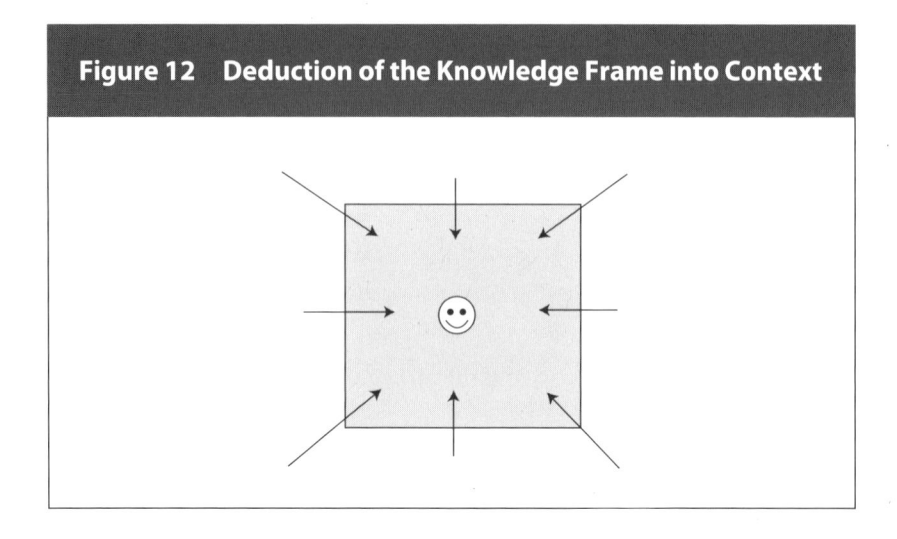

Figure 12   Deduction of the Knowledge Frame into Context

This mutual exchange in social groups is designed to inspire and encourage participants to think in new pathways of action about how governmental systems can be improved (2.1.2, 3.3.1). It requires that the individual learning actor be disposed to take a chance and to think in new or alternative knowledge patterns that are related to the potential forthcoming actions (2.3.1, 2.3.2). It also establishes a new peer-to-peer relationship, in which none of the participants wants to stay behind and miss the opportunity to be the first to introduce new and promising governmental changes (2.3.2).

In this transformation stage, the learning actors screen the new knowledge frame in regard to specific measures that are helping improve their governmental systems. In this step, these new insights get validated and improved in a peer review and are subsequently translated into a concrete action plan. This plan foresees all steps, which have to be considered to implement the gained knowledge into the actual individual and organizational governmental environment.

Stage 8: Configuration

Following the previous four steps, the newly reframed knowledge (induction) and its contextual transformation (deduction) have to be configured, under the direction of the event facilitator, into written summaries, transcripts, audio and video tapes, and so forth to be available to the learning actors (2.2.2). The developed material must be further complemented with the description of the event procedures in order to make the learning process comprehensible, transparent, and verifiable (2.3.1, 2.3.2).

Because governments worldwide deal with comparable challenges, the developed materials should be made available to other countries and their governmental and nongovernmental organizations (see Figure 13 and subsections 2.1.1 and 2.1.2). These potential users, however, should be alerted that the knowledge is normative in nature and therefore needs first to be adapted according to the contextual needs of a given governmental environment before being applied (2.2.1). To make the materials accessible for such an international audience, they have to be distributed by all means of communication, such as Web sites, blogs, and other types of social media. And last, because knowledge in democratic governance has a short half-life, its distribution has to be done quickly to remain relevant for potential users (2.2.1, 3.2.2).

To ensure that the new knowledge frame does not lose its relevance for practitioners, it has to be reviewed on a regular basis (2.2.1, 2.3.2, 3.2.2). If there is evidence that it is not relevant anymore, it needs to be reprocessed swiftly in a new spin of the Learning Spiral (2.1.1). In this case the knowledge developed through the learning process becomes the basis on which the new knowledge frame will be selected and processed (3.2.2).

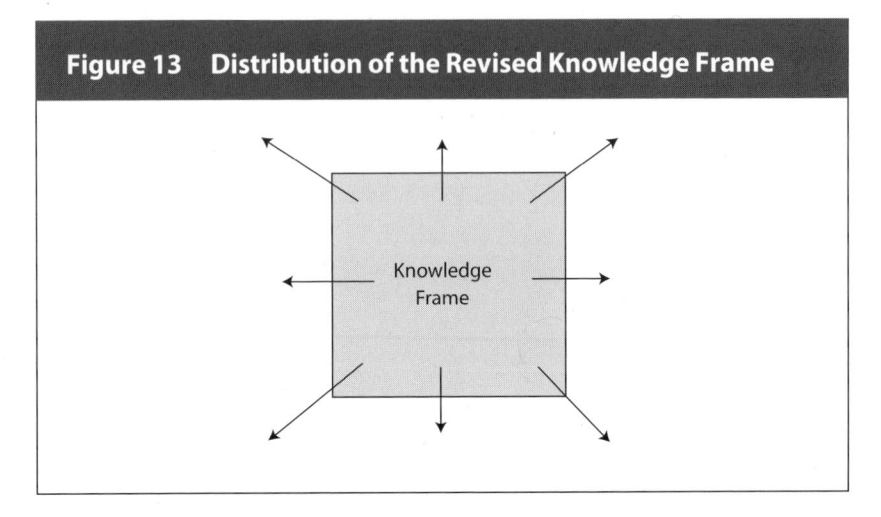

Figure 13　Distribution of the Revised Knowledge Frame

In the final configuration stage, the developed knowledge has to be summarized in an easy accessible format and distributed to the participants as well as to an interested international audience.

4.3 Practice of the Learning Spiral

For the Learning Spiral to be functional, it has to be organized in a template that defines all measures that make it applicable in a particular governmental learning event. Its concrete practice is initiated and realized by an event facilitator, who also ensures the further development of the Learning Spiral as well as its longer-term evaluation, which is based on a newly developed results framework.

4.3.1 Template and Organization

To make the eight stages of the Learning Spiral concept ready for practical use, they all have to be operationalized in a template that is applicable to any sort of governmental learning event. In this template the stages are aligned in a chronological order and split into three distinct sequences, which have to be carried through before, during, and after a particular learning activity (see Figure 14).

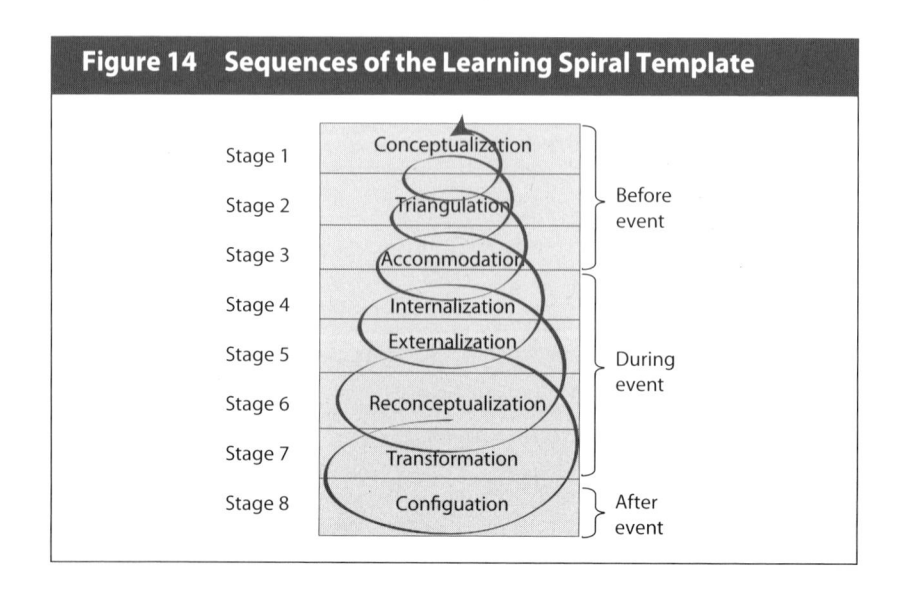

Figure 14 Sequences of the Learning Spiral Template

Stage	Phase	Sequence
Stage 1	Conceptualization	Before event
Stage 2	Triangulation	Before event
Stage 3	Accommodation	Before event
Stage 4	Internalization	During event
Stage 5	Externalization	During event
Stage 6	Reconceptualization	During event
Stage 7	Transformation	During event
Stage 8	Configuration	After event

1. The conceptualization, triangulation, and accommodation stages are considered as the preparatory stages, where the knowledge to be learned is framed, the selection and invitation of the participants is completed, and an initial bond and a sense of trust between the learning actors and the event facilitator and between participants and the learning process is established.
2. The internalization, externalization, reconceptualization, and transformation stages represent the core of the didactical procedures, where the learning actors review and adapt the new knowledge according to their personal needs. Thereafter the actors change their individual and organizational thinking and behavior in an elaborate inter- and intrapersonal procedure accordingly.
3. The follow-up to the learning activity is organized in the final configuration stage, where all developed knowledge is made available and accessible to everybody involved in the learning activity as well as to a wider audience. This new knowledge further serves as the knowledge frame of the next spin of the Learning Spiral, as well as a feedback loop in the context of a new learning system.

Because knowledge in public governance has a short half-life and has to be replaced in an ongoing manner, the learning process itself has to be ongoing, too. This iterative procedure, where knowledge is constantly reviewed, renewed, and transformed into political action in a real-time, multi-turn process, can be illustrated as a spiral. In a figurative way, each of the eight stages of the learning process is bound together by a spin, which ends with the last configuration stage and restarts the next spin with the consecutive first stage (see Figure 14).[9]

The Learning Spiral template does not allow mechanical application of the different learning stages. Instead, the concept has to be applied on a case-by-case base depending on the kind of knowledge to be learned as well as the governmental circumstances in which the event is taking place. The template represents a comprehensive guideline that provides directions for how an effective and appropriate learning activity has to be designed and carried through. However, as will be demonstrated with

---

9. This mechanism of a spiral in ongoing motion led to the term Learning Spiral.

the application of the Learning Spiral in five selected learning events (see chapters 5–9), there are always political, financial, and/or logistical constraints that limit implementation of the concept. In such cases, deliberate decisions have to be made regarding which compromises are tolerable and do not jeopardize an optimal performance of the learning process as a whole.

Such decisions are the authority of the facilitator who oversees all the event-related activities. This newly created independent and nonpartisan role, called the *learning broker*,[10] is in charge of all responsibilities that are traditionally overtaken by an event organizer, who is in charge of the event operations, and the moderator, who leads the event proceedings. With this new function, the number of directly engaged roles is reduced from the traditional four—the event organizer, moderator, speaker, and participants—to just two: the learning actors and the learning broker (see subsection 2.2.2).

The reason to bring together this wide set of tasks under the responsibility of one authority lies in the comprehensive nature of the Learning Spiral. In this type of learning activity, where the participants are knowledge recipients and knowledge holders alike, the content-related event procedures as well as the quality of offered logistical services have to be closely interrelated and should therefore not be separated. Accordingly, the quality of information and operational services has to fulfill the exact same criteria as the role speakers in traditional learning events take (see subsection 2.2.3).

The major responsibilities of the learning broker include the following tasks, enumerated in the order they are performed: framing the knowledge; facilitating its ongoing revision to maintain its practical relevance; selecting, inviting, and briefing the knowledge holders and the institutional stakeholders; providing a trustworthy learning environment that includes physical security and logistical comfort; designing the agenda; moderating the interactive learning procedures; enforcing the event proceedings and the communication rules; and finally, facili-

---

10. The term of the *learning broker* was first introduced by Rose (1991) and then by Dolowitz and Marsh (2000). The understanding of the term is largely derived from Matthew Andrews' theoretical description of the *external development expert* in his *network connector* model (Andrews 2008b, Andrews et al. 2010).

tating accessibility of the newly developed knowledge to both participants and a wider audience.

Fulfilling this wide range of tasks requires a broad set of skills: The learning broker needs detailed knowledge about the content to be learned so that he or she can frame it and select the participants accordingly. For that purpose he or she needs an extensive network in the field. Furthermore, he or she has to have high levels of social competency and communicative abilities to lead the dialogue within broad multi-stakeholder networks. And last, the learning broker has to have the creative capabilities to both design appropriate event structures according to the knowledge at stake and set up the operational and procedural steps.

To properly perform this comprehensive set of tasks, the learning broker depends on an institution that secures the iterative process as well as the long-term development of the Learning Spiral. This kind of learning agency can be a multilateral donor such as the World Bank, a national development organization, or a think tank that has a sustainable presence and a broad network. Besides providing the support for the learning brokers' activities, these agencies are also responsible for the longer-term management of the learning process. Thus, they not only ensure a particular government's ongoing development in an iterative procedure, but they simultaneously update and review their own knowledge inventory with the latest and most accurate trends and experiences made in the field.

This ongoing feedback loop allows the learning agencies to adapt and transform their own organizational policies and strategies accordingly. To secure and develop the quality of the Learning Spiral, it is the agency's duty to evaluate the performance of the concept itself and if necessary to refine and improve the design of the template.

In summary, compared with traditional learning events, the organization of the Learning Spiral template in a governmental learning activity requires a change of paradigm on multiple levels (see Table 5).

Learning agencies that use traditional learning settings tend to deliver explicit and normative knowledge, taught by experts on a given subject. In contrast, the concept of the Learning Spiral foresees that the knowledge to be learned includes explicit as well as tacit knowledge and combines normative and situative aspects, which are selected by the learning broker and exchanged among the learning actors in an inter-

Table 5 Comparison of Different Levels of Organization

	Traditional Concepts	Learning Spiral
Type of knowledge	Explicit and normative	Explicit and tacit Normative and situative
Knowledge intermediator	Expert	Learning broker
Didactics	Teaching	Interactive dialogue
Target audience	Many and unselected	Few and selected
Goal of learning	Change of state of knowledge (factual)	Change of behavior (meaning/understanding)

active dialogue. In traditional concepts the goal of learning is to update the state of knowledge of as many as possible participants. The purpose of the learning process is to change the behavior of a few selected participants in an intended direction. In the conventional learning model, knowledge is transmitted in the form of concrete facts; in the Learning Spiral process, the focus of the learning effort is on understanding the meaning of a particular set of knowledge.

This last conclusion has profound implications for measuring the success of learning: In traditional concepts, the amount of knowledge gained is measurable right at the end of a learning activity through an evaluation of the new knowledge retained by each participant. In contrast, the results of the Learning Spiral process have to be observed over time by evaluating individual and organizational behavioral changes.

4.3.2 Evaluation and Results Framework[11]

Though the Learning Spiral has been developed and applied over the last decade, it has yet to be rigorously evaluated and grounded in a *results framework*.[12] To improve the concept continuously, a clear definition of its

---

11. This *results framework* has been developed and edited by Bidjan Nashat.
12. A *results framework* describes the chain of inputs, activities, outputs, outcomes, and impacts of a project, program, or policy. In combination with a theory of change, it lays out a causal chain and shows the key assumptions and beliefs about why a project, program, or policy is likely to reach its objectives. Inputs are defined as resources that

intended results and more rigorous evaluation methods will help further improve its quality. The difficulty of measuring such complex operations and procedures lies partly in the fact that the short, medium-, and long-term results of efforts in governmental learning are difficult to attribute.

The Learning Spiral concept already has a sound foundation from a theoretical and an empirical perspective. It is grounded in several theories, all of which have been developed and tested successfully. Each of these theories and their hypotheses are the result of long-lasting and highly renowned research. The empirical evidence of the concept is based on evaluations that were made at the end of all learning events where the Learning Spiral was applied.[13] These Level One evaluations measure the reaction of the participants and what they think and feel about the event right after the activities end.[14] In addition, several impact reports by selected high-level participants show how the event triggered reflections, learning, and behavioral and organizational change on different levels over time.[15]

The combination of empirical evaluative knowledge from Level One (participant responses), evidence from Levels Three and Four (behavioral change and organizational impact), and selected evidence from reflections on its application mentioned above provide a theoretical and empirical starting point for developing a results framework for the Learning Spiral as part of the learning system.

However, the theoretical foundation and the existing evaluations of selected applications of the Learning Spiral provide necessary but insufficient evidence for its longer-term impact. Previous evaluations did not focus

---

go into a project, program, or policy, whereas activities describe what is being done (in this case, applying the Learning Spiral). Outputs are usually tangible products or services, but access and awareness can be defined as outputs as well. Outcomes can usually be increased, enhanced, or improved. Impacts are the long-term changes that result from an accumulation of outcomes (Morra Imas and Rist 2009).
13. For a recent and representative example of such a participant's evaluation, see *Workshop Findings: Lessons of a Decade of Public Sector Reform* (IEG 2008e).
14. This Level One evaluation is part of a comprehensive evaluation model developed by Donald Kirkpatrick (1998) that comprises three additional consecutive levels. They are Level Two, which measures the increase in knowledge or capability; Level Three, which measures the extent of behavioral and capability improvement and implementation/application; and Level Four, which measures the effects on the organization and its environment resulting from the participant's behavioral change.
15. See, for example, Boxes 1–6 in chapters 5–9.

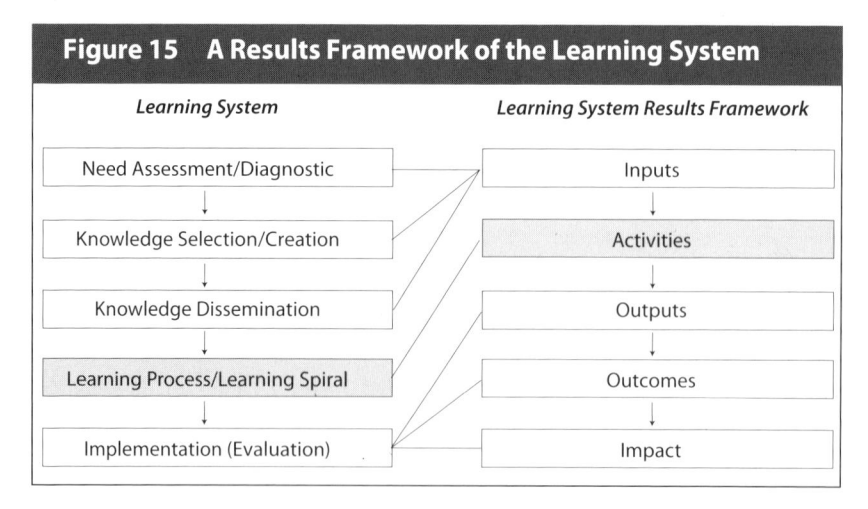

Figure 15 A Results Framework of the Learning System

Learning System	Learning System Results Framework
Need Assessment/Diagnostic	Inputs
Knowledge Selection/Creation	Activities
Knowledge Dissemination	Outputs
Learning Process/Learning Spiral	Outcomes
Implementation (Evaluation)	Impact

on the whole learning system, from its initial need assessment to implementation, and thus could not assess the results of its longer-term application.

Therefore, developing a comprehensive results framework is an important requirement for determining the Learning Spiral's impact, because the framework describes the causal steps of how the application of the concept contributes to the implementation of a given set of knowledge in democratic governance. It begins with a definition of its goal directions or its impacts, outcomes, outputs, activities, and inputs.[16] Outputs are characterized as what is being produced as a result of the activities, whereas outcomes are the behavioral changes resulting from the project outputs and impacts are the long-term changes that result from an accumulation of outcomes (Morra Imas and Rist 2009).

Developing this framework also requires an explanation of how the Learning Spiral functions as a part of the learning system. The learning process, in which the Learning Spiral's stages are applied, represents the missing link between knowledge dissemination and implementation in the learning system (subsection 4.1.1). Thus, as elaborated in previous chapters (subsection 4.1.2), the Learning Spiral ties into the former black box of the learning system as an activity in the results framework (see Figure 15).

---

16. The literature on capacity building mentions different approaches for how to determine the achievement in complex systems. Among them are Otoo et al. (2009), Blindenbacher (1997), Parsons (1951), and Kusek and Rist (2004).

In a results framework, all official and operative goals have to be taken into consideration. With regard to the inputs, there is a distinction between content and process. The content-related input consists of the first three steps of the learning system—needs assessment/diagnostic, knowledge selection/creation, and knowledge dissemination. The resource-related inputs are the learning broker's skills, event logistics, and operational resources. The eight stages of the Learning Spiral constitute the activities in the results framework. The application of the Learning Spiral's eight stages produces three outputs and outcomes:

1. *Implementation of action plans:* The most important output of the Learning Spiral's application is an increased awareness of the combination of normative and situative knowledge among learning actors and a specific action plan for adaptation in the local context. The action plan exemplifies the willingness of the learning actors to implement the intended results. Following the output, the outcome of the Learning Spiral is defined as a contribution to visible behavioral change in governments in the intended direction as a result of the adapted knowledge, thereby closing the link between knowledge dissemination and implementation in the learning system.[17] This outcome assumes that if all necessary learning actors have been included in the learning event and their awareness of the normative and situative knowledge has been raised, the chances for subsequent behavioral change in their governments increase.[18]

2. *Re-evaluation/Updating of knowledge:* The second output of the Learning Spiral's application manifests itself in reviewed and revised set of knowledge that combines the normative and situative knowledge for the learning actors.[19] Moving this output into an outcome requires a successful feedback loop, in which the newly developed knowledge is used in the next learning activity—in the next spin of the Learning Spiral. For learning agencies the constant updating of knowledge through learning events thus offers the chance to reflect

---

17. See Boxes 1–6 in the chapters 5–9 for past evidence on this outcome.
18. For a similar approach to learning outcomes that centers on the role of change agents in capacity development, see the WBI's Capacity Development Results Framework (Otoo et al. 2009).
19. See, for example, the Level One evaluation from the learning event in *Workshop Findings: Lessons of a Decade of Public Sector Reform* (IEG 2008e).

and evaluate the organizations' own state-of-the-art knowledge and to adapt organizational policies and strategies accordingly.

3. *The creation of networks:* Achieving the third output of the Learning Spiral's application takes place through an increased connection and awareness of international network opportunities among learning actors as a result of continuous learning events. The outcome is meant to be a network of learning actors who engage in sustainable knowledge exchange. In this case, the newly gained knowledge is used to feed the next spin of a learning process and enable a network of actors to engage in a continuous dialogue about solutions for democratic governance.[20]

Taken together, the three outcomes of the Learning Spiral should lead to one major impact: the improvement of the overall quality of a democratic governmental system. This includes in particular the implementation of a comprehensive set of democratic principles and the delivery of public services and public goods that match citizens' needs and expectations and that also shape and lead the appropriate governmental institutions (see subsections 2.1.1 and 3.2.2).

This results framework explains the key causal assumptions on how the Learning Spiral leads to outputs, outcomes, and impact. For future evaluations of the Learning Spiral's results, the existing literature on evaluating the inputs, activities, outputs, and outcomes of learning define a wide array of indicators and methods that could be adjusted and operationalized for monitoring and evaluating the effectiveness of each step in this results framework.[21]

---

20. For a more detailed definition and indicators on the learning outcome of fostering networks and coalitions, see the WBI's Capacity Development Results Framework (Otoo et al. 2009).

21. Among them are the World Bank Institute's Capacity Development Results Framework (Otoo et al. 2009), IEG's evaluation of the World Bank's project-based and WBI's training activities (IEG 2008a), and the handbook for public-private dialogue by Herzberg and Wright (2006). For more qualitative methods, see the indicators for evaluating deliberative public engagement developed by Gastil (2009).

Part II: Practical Application

To showcase the Learning Spiral's practical application in concrete governmental learning events, its implementation is demonstrated in five different types of learning settings: an international conference (chapter 5); a multiyear, global program with national and international roundtables (chapter 6); a study tour (chapter 7); an evaluation-based workshop (chapter 8); and a multimedia training and e-learning initiative (chapter 9). The case studies were deliberately chosen to prove the Learning Spiral's applicability in a wide range of governmental learning activities. Each example is introduced by a detailed description of the event organization, followed by the presentation of the operations and procedures according to the eight stages of the Learning Spiral template. Final comments, including the results of the events evaluation findings, wrap up each case study. For further illustration the studies are supplemented by six firsthand accounts written by participants who describe their learning experiences.

5 International Conference

The first application of the Learning Spiral on an international scale was at the Second International Conference on Federalism, held in St. Gallen, Switzerland, in 2002. This four-day conference was a follow-up event to a conference held in 1999 in Canada. In the first event the proceedings were structured to maximize learning from world leaders and international experts; the second conference, in contrast, focused primarily on the participants' experiences.[1]

The aim of the 2002 event was to provide a forum for the exchange of ideas and experiences among practitioners of federalism from politics, civil service, academia, culture, corporate business, and other spheres of society. The Swiss federal and cantonal governments shared the basic costs of the event. The audience was composed of 600 participants from 60 countries, who were interested in a constructive exchange of experiences and information in the field of federal governance. The learning-oriented dialogue was directed to develop new federal problem-solving models, which are supposed to take into account worldwide change (General Information Brochure 2002).

5.1 Conference Reader—Conceptualization Stage

A board of directors composed of eminent Swiss nationals and a few international experts who had been involved in the organization of the first conference supervised the strategic planning of the 2002 event. A broad consortium of international practitioners and scholars directed the content preparation. For all other operational and procedural responsibilities, a project manager

---

[1]. Among the most eminent speakers of the first conference were President Bill Clinton of the United States, President Ernesto Zedillo of Mexico, and the Prime Minister of Canada, Jean Chretien. For an overview of the past and forthcoming International Conferences on Federalism, see Raoul Blindenbacher and Rupak Chattopadhyay (2007).

(learning broker) was in charge. This individual had been hired two years prior to the event and completed the work one year after the conference.[2]

To narrow the broad topic of federal governance and to make it manageable for the intended learning process of the second conference, the conference organizers determined a common understanding of the subject and selected a set of internationally relevant conference themes. The chosen themes were federalism and foreign policy; federalism, decentralization, and conflict management in multicultural societies; and assignment of responsibilities and fiscal federalism.[3] To lay a solid groundwork of the knowledge to be learned and to provide possible solutions, a group of well-known international experts on federalism prepared concise papers regarding each theme. The content included a rationale of the theme selection, a summary of the state-of-the-art research in the field, and key questions to assist the in-depth consideration of particular cases in the conference sessions.

The authors presented the papers for the first time at a preconference, held six months before the conference. The papers were extensively discussed and validated by the authors and the conference organizers. At the preconference, the conference moderators, who had been selected to facilitate the different sessions at the main event, also attended. The purpose of this was to familiarize them with the state-of-the-art knowledge on each theme and to make sure that they understood their particular role as well as the conference process. The reviewed papers were published in a conference reader (Abderhalden and Blindenbacher 2002) and also made available on the conference Web site.[4] The conference readers were distributed two months prior to the main conference so the participants could be properly prepared for the upcoming event.

---

2. For all logistical matters and the practical realization of the conference, the project manager was supported by the International Students committee (ISC), an independent initiative of students at the University of St. Gallen. For further information about the ISC, see www.stgallen-symposium.org.
3. For a rationale of how the themes were selected, see Raoul Blindenbacher and Ronald Watts (2003).
4. The conference Web site was closed at the time of publication of this book. Its content was transferred to the Web site of the Forum of Federations: www.forumfed.org.

5.2 Sixty Federal and Decentralized Countries— Triangulation Stage

The heart of the conference consisted of four-hour work sessions, which were introduced through case studies illustrating the different aspects of the theme concerned. To present the fullest possible picture of a given case, the content needed to be explored from a number of different reference points. Therefore, during the work sessions the cases (up to five) were presented by three to five individuals in short summaries detailing their responses to the questions formulated in the papers. The presenters were deliberately not chosen according to the positions they held, but according to themes and interests. All 24 work sessions held at the conference, 8 for each theme, followed this pattern.

One example that illustrates this pattern well was the work session about the theme of Assignment of Responsibilities and Fiscal Federalism. This theme had a corresponding subtheme: Problems of Equalization in Federal Systems. Fiscal equalization refers to attempts within a federal system of government to reduce fiscal disparities among jurisdictions. It is qualified as vertical when the policy is conducted by a central government and financed by the central budget. It is horizontal when it intervenes between government units at the same level, through monetary transfers from units with *high* to units with *low* capacity.

For triangulation purposes, three cases were selected to represent a vertical, a horizontal, and a hybrid type of equalization. The vertical model was illustrated by Australia, the horizontal type by Canada, and the hybrid type by Switzerland. The case presenters were a head of state, a federal minister, and a director of state government, respectively. Thus, three additional distinctive perspectives, representing different levels of executive government, were added to the mix of possible viewpoints regarding this theme.

This broad selection of different country cases, presented from different angles, allowed a comprehensive and unique understanding of the session subthemes. Copying this pattern to the 24 other work session made it possible for almost all 60 countries to present at least one case, and more than two-thirds of the participants had a prepared assignment to share their individual perspective.

5.3 Introduction of the Conference Reader— Accommodation Stage

To provide the best possible learning conditions, deliberate steps of trust building were pursued long before the conference began. On the content side, the selected knowledge was made accessible to everybody involved into the learning event. In regard to the learning process itself, participants were individually informed and updated about the conference agenda and the participants list, as well as the particular role they were expected to perform. The selection criteria for invitations were accessible and transparent. Most important among them was the rule that only primary stakeholders were invited and no self-acting replacements were accepted.

The whole conference was set up so that every participant got similar treatment. Because a dozen of the participants were heads of state, the general care of participants had to be very attentive and personal. There was a 24-hour helpdesk where the organizers offered support for participant requests. To give everybody the opportunity to know who was who, the participants got an electronic device that allowed them to identify other participants around them.[5] This device also permitted the organizers to communicate with all or selected participants to inform them about general news or changes in the program.

The high number of dignitaries made a high level of security indispensable. However, for the comfort of the participants, there were no visible security measures in the conference compound. Security was as discreet as possible, and participants were free to move around and to approach whomever they wanted. Furthermore, there was no formal seating during any events, including meals or the different conference sessions.

In such an equalizing design, it was crucial to establish well-communicated and strictly enforced communication rules. Most important were the Chatham House Rules, which guaranteed that participants would not quote each other without permission.[6] This rule was also standard

---

5. For further information about the device, see http://www.spotme.com/.
6. When a meeting is held under the Chatham House Rules, participants are free to use the information received, but neither the identity nor the affiliation of the speaker(s), nor that of any other participant, may be revealed. For further information see http://www.chathamhouse.org.uk/.

for journalists, who were obliged to sign a nondisclosure document. During the conference sessions it was the moderator's duty to assert the dialogue rules, such as speaking time limits, which in general were not to exceed five minutes. English was the general working language, but to facilitate communications, there were six official conference languages with simultaneous translation in the plenary sessions.

5.4 Work Sessions—Internalization Stage

As mentioned above, the center of the conference was the 24 parallel work sessions, which were held once in the morning of the second day and once on the third conference day. Four of the twelve sessions were dedicated to one of the three themes, each with a slightly different focus. Each work session was set up as a roundtable, with no front table or podium. It was not discernable which speakers were the designated speakers and which were not. The work sessions were led by a moderator who oversaw and handled the program procedures, such as setting the order of speakers, introducing speakers, and setting breaks. The moderator was responsible for ensuring that the discussion did not stray from the given theme, that the communication rules were reinforced, and that all participants had a fair chance to take part in the proceedings and contribute to the dialogue.

In all, 15 moderators were carefully selected according to their skills in group dynamics, assertiveness, conflict management, and an ability to instill enthusiasm—as well as according to formal criteria such as nationality and gender. Particular attention was also given to their records in dealing with different cultures. They all had extensive experience in facilitating political dialogues at the highest international level. To ensure impartiality, they were expected not to be actively associated with special-interest groups. The selected facilitators had proven an extensive interest in political matters. To update their know-how about the given topic, they were all required to participate at the preconference.

Each work session was introduced through cases illustrating the theme concerned; these cases served as a starting point for the learning-oriented dialogue. The cases were described in one-page fact sheets, which were distributed to the participants the first day of the conference. According to the triangulation procedure, the cases were introduced in short summaries by selected participants, detailing their responses to the questions formulated in the papers. The selection of the speakers was made according to the specific perspective they brought to the table. It was important that as a group they represented different political levels as well as diverse spheres of society. Furthermore, they had to be recognized key players in their fields. These statements provided the vital link between theory and practice and ensured that the ensuing dialogue had its foundations in existing situations and problems.

In the example of problems of equalization in federal systems, the questions raised in the theme paper were about the issue of who funded the equalization system and who received the funding, and based on what criteria. The Australian, Canadian, and Swiss speakers were briefed to answer the questions as completely as possible, providing both positive and negative comments. Thus their presentations became the point on which to engage the other participants in the learning process; that is, others would follow their example by analyzing their own country situation in the light of the questions raised. The rationale of the presentations was therefore—besides the obvious purpose of valuable knowledge transfer—to build trust and confidence among the participants as they reflected on their own situations in an honest manner.

The design of the work sessions entitled the *Dialogue Leaders* to draw on a set of selected participants who had a designated role (see Figure 16 and Photo 1).

Figure 16 Work Session Set Up
Photo 1   Work Session Roundtable

Note: DL = Dialogue Leader; WC = Work Session Chair; CP = Case Presenter; SE = Scientific Expert; YP = Young Professional; SW = Scientific Summary Writer.

Among these roles was—besides the *Case Presenters*—the *Work Session Chair*, whose role involved the introduction of the participants. The presence of the Chair also provided the sessions with a necessary element of formality, as dignitaries of the highest political level were among the participants. It was important that their function in government stood in a direct relation to the theme of the session. The moderators were further assisted by the authors of the theme papers: their role as *Scientific Experts* in the field and their academic knowledge enabled them to place contributions by the practitioners in a theoretical and generalized framework, putting the dialogue in a new perspective and opening up new areas.

Another role was the *Young Professional*. These individuals were expected to make statements about the questions from a perspective focusing on anticipated challenges and their methods of resolution. The Young Professionals had to be younger than 30 and were selected based on the quality of papers they had submitted prior to the conference.

And last there were the *Scientific Summary Writers*, whose role involved summing up the work sessions, paraphrasing the dialogue, and undertaking an initial analysis of its content. The writers were selected according to their academic skills in regard to the theme as well as their proven journalistic and editing skills. Together with the moderator, the scientific summary writers were the only individuals sitting at the roundtable who explicitly did not engage in the dialogue.

5.5 Dialogue Tables—Externalization Stage

The forum was held in *dialogue tables*.[7] These tables were convened early in the afternoon of the second and third days of the conference, held after the work sessions conducted in the morning. There were three parallel dialogue table sessions, each dedicated to one of the three themes. These sessions allowed an intense interactive session devoted to small groups in which the dividing line between the speakers and those listening was deliberately removed. To this end, the participants investigating

---

7. *Dialogue tables* are a didactical forum inspired by Harrison Owen's (1997) open space concept. For a detailed description and theoretical explanation, see Raoul Blindenbacher et al. (2001).

the same theme were brought together in a large room, divided into small groups of eight, and seated at small tables. The dialogue tables were led by a moderator whose task was to familiarize the participants with the method, to lay down the given time frame, and make sure the session proceeded properly (see Figures 17–19).

In the first phase, the case presenters were gathered around bar tables on a small podium, where they were asked to succinctly summarize the knowledge they personally had gained from the preceding work session. Once collected, these statements gave the participants on the floor an impression of the direction in which new problem-solving models and—where appropriate—a new understanding of the theme could develop (see Figure 17 and Photo 2).

Following a brief session in which the audience had the opportunity to ask questions, the podium speakers were each asked to join one of the dialogue tables. It was important to ensure that at least one speaker was allocated to each table. In this second phase, each table had to validate the statements made and to contrast them with the individual experiences of the participants at that table. It was particularly important to reflect as a group on questions about the new knowledge and where it fit in each individual's experience. A rotation system was used to stimulate the dialogue tables, whereby the podium speakers had to leave their table and join a new one (see Figure 18 and Photo 3) at regular intervals.

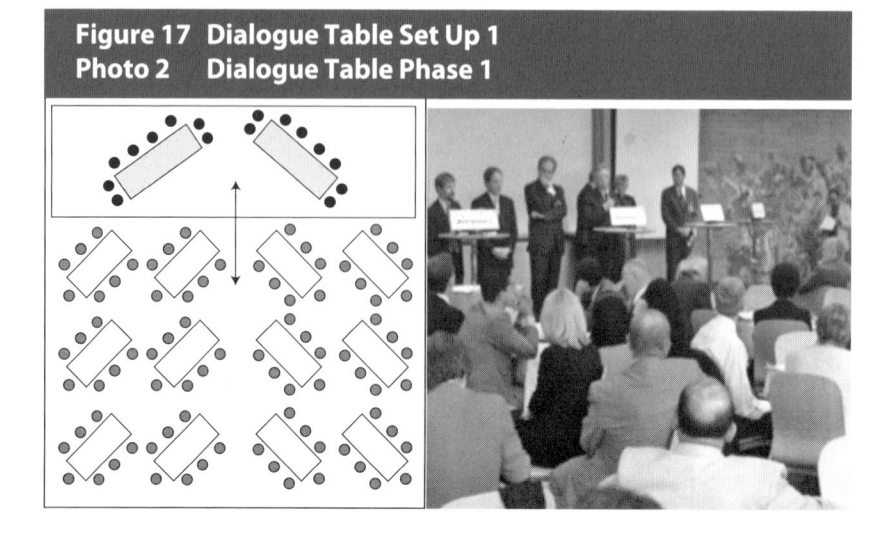

Figure 17   Dialogue Table Set Up 1
Photo 2   Dialogue Table Phase 1

Figure 18 Dialogue Table Set Up 2
Photo 3   Dialogue Table Phase 2

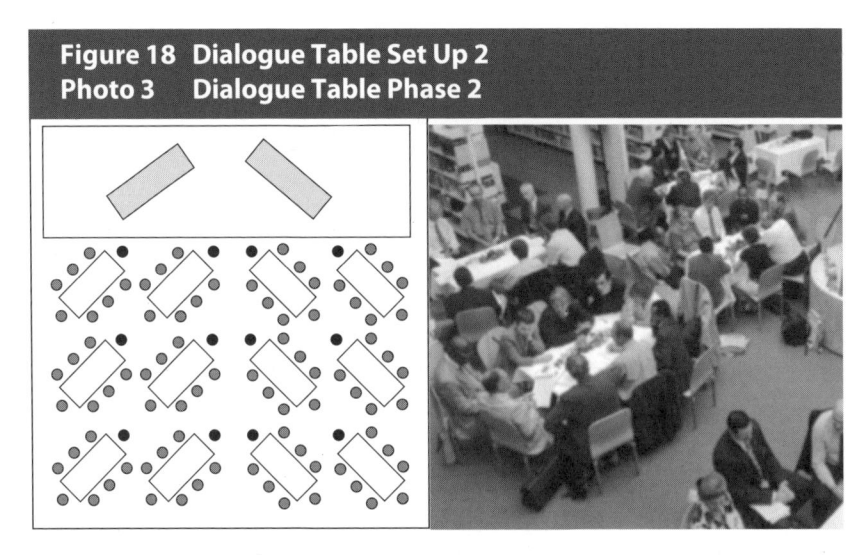

In the third and final phase, one participant (*not* the podium speakers) from each table was asked to share with all the participants the most important information they had acquired from the group dialogues (see Figure 19 and Photo 4).

To capture the essential content of the dialogue table sessions, several scientific summary writers paraphrased all the statements made by the presenters in the first and third session phases and summarized them in a comprehensive paper.

Figure 19 Dialogue Table Set Up 3
Photo 4   Dialogue Table Phase 3

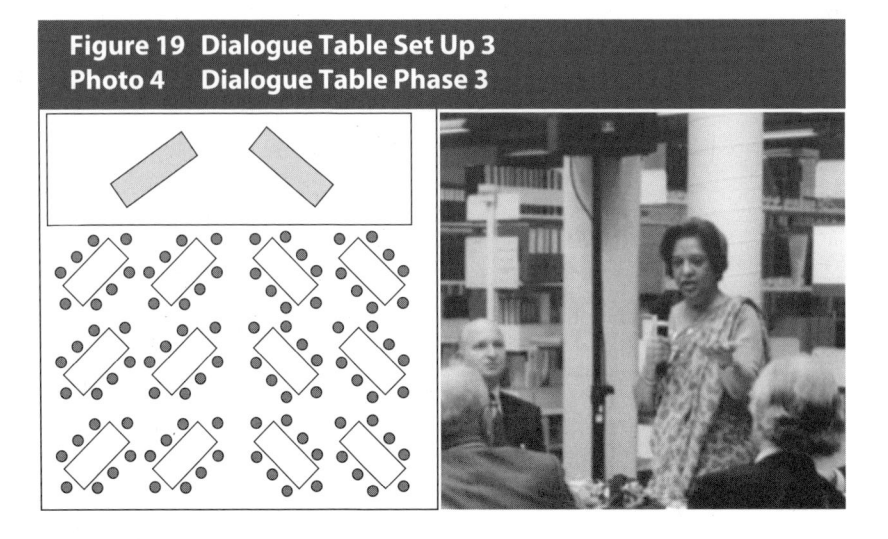

5.6 Expert Summaries—Reconceptualization Stage

On the fourth and last conference day, the authors of the three original theme papers in their concluding remarks outlined new insights and emerging trends that they had observed over the course of the work sessions and dialogue tables. In these presentations they framed the lessons learned as well as new patterns from a theoretical perspective and extrapolated their impact on each of the three themes. All the speakers of the interactive plenary panels were advised to make their presentations as freely and spontaneously as possible. The conference organizers had offered to the speakers a team of advisors who helped them finalize their presentations.

5.7 Interactive Plenary Panels—Transformation Stage

In the final conference session, selected heads of government and state were asked in an interactive plenary panel to react to the proposed new thematic outlines presented in the previous session. They were invited to share their thoughts on how the newly framed knowledge could impact their respective countries and to what extent they could anticipate implementing some of these new considerations in their own political strategies. By asking eminent participants to do this, conference organizers expected that the issues raised by the speakers would get additional attention among the other participants and would thus motivate them to follow their example (see Photo 5).

Photo 5 Interactive Plenary Session

(From left to right) Belgium Prime Minister Guy Verhofstadt, former Swiss President Arnold Koller, former Yugoslavian President Vojislav Kostunica, and Austrian Chancellor Wolfgang Schuessel

In the second part of the final session, the participants were encouraged to comment on and complement the issues raised by the previous speakers and to exchange their thoughts how the new state-of-the-art knowledge could end up being transformed and implemented in their own particular political environment.

A rather unexpected side effect of the conference was that a number of participating countries ended up organizing national follow-up events, where the application of the newly gained knowledge was further discussed in the context of the respective countries.

5.8 Conference Proceedings—Configuration Stage

Shortly after the conference, the authors of the theme papers revised their original documents according to the results of the conference process. Concurrently the scientific summary writers finalized their notes about the work sessions and dialogue table proceedings, and the plenary speakers edited their speeches from the interactive plenary panels. Subsequently, all this material was archived by the conference organizers and published in a conference book (Blindenbacher and Koller 2003), as well as made available on the conference Web site.

In a final step, the publication was sent to every participant and was made available in bookstores for the public. However, and most important, its content became the background material for the third and fourth International Conferences on Federalism, held in Brussels, Belgium, in 2005, and in New Delhi, India, in 2007. Thus the new knowledge in federal governance became the basis for the newly selected content to be learned in a next spin of the Learning Spiral process.

5.9 Final Comments and Evaluation

The Second International Conference on Federalism was the first major event where the eight stages of the Learning Spiral template were almost fully applied. The conditions under which the conference was organized were exceptional: The conference management was well staffed and funded, and it had all the necessary political support to do its work freely and independently. The time frame of almost three years from the first planning until the publication of the conference proceedings was sufficient to properly carry through all tasks for each stage and allowed a well-carried-out transition to the follow-up events in Brussels and New Delhi. The direct involvement with the follow-up events paid off particularly well because the new conference organizers adopted the same learning concept, which in turn secured the continuity of the learning process.[8]

The conference was rated by a Level One evaluation (see subsection 4.3.2): 81 percent of the participants appraised the overall quality of the event in regard to content and organization as excellent, and 19 percent rated it as good. Ninety-one percent appraised the quality of the dialogue in the work sessions as excellent, as did 88 percent for the interactive plenary sessions and 70 percent for the dialogue tables. More than 250 participant letters and e-mails sent after the conference are testimony to the impressive level of substance at the event (Koller 2003). This positive impression about the event appears to have been long lasting, as reflected in two testimonies made eight years after the event was held: one is written from a participant who was involved in the subtheme on fiscal equalization (see Box 1) and one discusses the learning process itself (see Box 2).

A last, rather surprising characteristic of the conference was that 92 percent of the confirmed participants ended up attending—even though many of them had to pay a conference fee as well their own travel costs. Possible explanations for this unusual occurrence include that most participants had a well-defined role to perform and therefore felt obliged to attend, and that nobody wanted to risk missing a unique opportunity to have access to and to learn about the latest knowledge on governance in federal systems.

---

8. For the description of the proceedings of the conference in Brussels, see Frank Geerkens (2005); for the New Delhi description, see Rupak Chattopadhyay et al. (2008).

Box 1 Reflections from the Deputy Chief Financial Officer and Chief Economist of the Washington, DC, Government

There are four fundamental questions of fiscal federalism: Which type of government performs which spending functions? Which government raises which revenues? When one adds up the franc (dinar, zloty, euro…) amounts in answering the first two questions and finds an expenditure-revenue gap for some local, cantonal, provincial, or municipal governments, how shall gap-closing intergovernmental transfers be designed and implemented? And fourth, what is the institutional setting within which the preceding questions are answered and implemented?

This note focuses on the third question the design of intergovernmental transfers, which was a subtheme at 2002 International Conference on Federalism of the dialogue and work sessions: Problems of Equalization in Federal Systems.

The capacity and willingness of governments to learn the topic of transfers is most important. For many federal systems, a well-designed system of intergovernmental transfers provides a vehicle for achieving a society's broader goals, which range from poverty reduction and the efficient delivery of public sector services to maintaining social cohesion and, for some countries, avoiding conflict. But if designed poorly, intergovernmental transfers worsen the fiscal position of local government and thus undermine or even undo the federal partnership.

To sort out the various policy and administrative options in answering the transfer question, there is a knowledge overlapping of (i) *own* country experience and (ii) sorting out the lessons of other countries (*learning from each other*). In the case of transfers, which was the major discussion point of the work session, the methodology of the Learning Spiral's eight stages provides a stylized framework for what, in practice, governments do if they are willing to institutionally and organizationally *learn*. For sure, the terminology will differ between the Learning Spiral and the practice of government. Thus, for example, the conceptualization through configuration stages of the Leaning Spiral may be thought of as a *sequencing* of tasks. This is not to suggest that either the eight stages or sequencing occur in a smooth step-by-step manner.

(Box continues on the following page.)

> **Box 1** *(continued)*
>
> There are many good books and conferences on the topic of intergovernmental transfers. But what makes the Learning Spiral important and different—as was demonstrated in its framing of the organization of the 2002 conference, which had a component of a large face-to-face convening activity in St. Gallen—was that it imposed the learning process on the content of the topic. In the case of the conference subtheme of fiscal equalization in the federal system, the content neatly mirrored the methodology of the triangulation step of the Learning Spiral. An equalization system can be qualified as (i) vertical when the policy is conducted by the central government and financed from the central budget; (ii) horizontal when the intervention is among governments, with the transfers being made from *high* to *low* fiscal capacity governments; or (ii) a hybrid of the first two. The vertical approach was illustrated by Australia, the horizontal by Canada, and the hybrid by Switzerland. When the participants in the conference met face to face in St. Gallen, the case presenters were a head of state, a federal minister, and a director of a cantonal government. Learning method, content, and institutions converge—voila!
>
> To be clear, the conference and the interface among learning methodology, content, and institutional practice were not just about St. Gallen. Rather, it was learning-from-each-other series of activities that, as with the content illustration above, *mapped* the Learning Spiral to a systematic set of knowledge sharing events. That is, the 2002 conference entailed much more than a *one-off* event whereby one convenes practitioners and policy makers for a few days of discussion. Rather, it was a series of learning stages that began with a series of *premeeting* knowledge-sharing activities, most electronically, which were followed by a series of electronic post-St. Gallen meetings and the publication of the conference book Federalism in a Changing World.
>
> Robert D. Ebel, Washington, DC, USA, March 5, 2010
>
> Robert D. Ebel Robert is currently Professor of Public Administration and Economics at the University of the District of Columbia.

Box 2 Reflections on the Conference Process from the Former Premier of Ontario and Current Member of the Parliament of Canada

The Second International Conference on Federalism at St. Gallen, Switzerland, took the Spiral of Learning concept to a new, practical level, where both the journey and the destination mattered. There was inevitably a tension between *experts* and *practitioners*, but that is in the nature of the beast, and both benefited from their necessarily different perspectives. The conference was a determined effort to put the medium and the message together. More rigorous structure and a greater effort at training facilitators meant that from the small group sessions to larger forums there was a constant effort to assemble conclusions and make sure debates and discussions didn't just drift off into the air (although there was inevitably some of that!).

One of my central beliefs is that the sharing of experiences provides one of the best ways for people to learn. What was happening in this conference was more than just conversation, or listening to speeches. It was at once more organized and focused than that, and took dialogue to a new level. The different work and dialogue sessions were forums in the true sense, a place where exchange and learning takes place. The idea was that practitioners needed to talk to each other, that those involved in the theory of federalism needed to talk to practitioners, and that young people needed to be brought into the mix to reinforce the sense that learning never stops and the next generation has an assured place at the table. The way federal governance got discussed in this event has been a reflection of the federal idea itself: a dialogue of equals, respectful, civil, around a common focus of interest. The principle of every exchange was to learn how to improve, based on the simple premise that we all have something to gain from an exchange that is at once focused and tries to reach conclusions.

The series of international conferences has now grown to a well-respected triennial event series whose participants span the globe, and whose venues—so far Canada, Belgium, Switzerland, India, and Ethiopia—reflect the same diversity. None of us, either individuals or countries or organizations, are islands unto ourselves. We learn from others, and that process of

(Box continues on the following page.)

> **Box 2** (*continued*)
>
> learning needs a little structure and discipline to be effective. Our mistakes can be even more important than our successes, and a real conversation around a common problem can be more effective than a self-indulgent speech. But the key to effectiveness is follow-up and follow-through, not just the epiphany of discovery, but seeing how discovery and insight can actually be applied in the real world—and how the effort of applying these insights itself produces new ways of seeing the world.
>
> Bob Rae, Toronto, Canada, December 21, 2009

6 Multiyear Global Program Roundtables

Though sharing experiences in federal governance may seem an obvious way to improve governmental systems and mechanisms, surprisingly, it has not been common practice. In an effort to create and deepen such learning processes, the Forum of Federations[1] and the International Association of Centers for Federal Studies[2] launched in 2002 the program "A Global Dialogue on Federalism." To date, the program has produced more than 80 national and international roundtables, held in 20 countries, with an active network of approximately 2,000 participants and a series of 6 published handbooks and 7 booklets.[3] The Canadian and the Swiss governments fund most of the program operations, which are conducted by a small staff provided by the Forum of Federations.

This learning activity entails a comparative exploration of different themes in federal governance.[4] In this learning process, new practical and theoretical knowledge is integrated with the aim of fostering a collective vision to develop new solutions for specific problems. These solutions are then transformed into measures producing practical action. The activities must further endeavor to build enduring cross-country contacts and a viable international network of practitioners and scholars interested in federalism. The way each theme is worked through follows the exact same procedure, which is designed on the basis of the Learning Spiral template (Blindenbacher and Saunders

---

1. For further information about the Forum of Federations, see www.forumfed.org.
2. For further information about the International Association of Centers for Federal Studies, see http://www.iacfs.org.
3. The handbook and booklet series are published by McGill-Queens University Press: www.mqup.ca.
4. For the nine themes dealt with to date, see the Global Dialogue's Program Web site: www.forumfed.org/en/global/gdparticipants.php.

2005; Blindenbacher and Brook 2005). For illustrative purposes, the theme Foreign Relations in Federal Countries, carried out from April until October 2006, was chosen to exemplify the program's learning procedure.

6.1 Theme Template—Conceptualization Stage

The Global Dialogue Program is overseen by an editorial board, which is composed of international experts on federal governance who provide policy and program guidance. This panel ensures that each theme is processed in the exact same way to ensure the consistency of the program. One further major task of the board is to select, in collaboration with the two sponsoring organizations, program themes.

This case study is of the board-proposed topic Foreign Relations in Federal Countries. This theme was considered particularly timely and challenging because constituent units in federal countries all over the world increasingly carry out relations with foreign governments at all levels. For the overall responsibility for the theme, the board appointed an international leading expert, referred to as the theme coordinator, whose major task was to draft a theme template. This template included an introduction that summarized the essence of the latest research and theory on the topic, a set of crosscutting analytical issues, and an internationally comprehensive set of questions covering institutional provisions and how they work in practice.

Among the most important issues explored in the template were questions such as the following:

- What constitutional powers do federal governments and constituent states have to conduct foreign affairs?
- To what degree are relations between orders of government regularized by formal agreements or informal practice?
- What roles do constituent governments have in negotiating and implementing international treaties?
- How are international activities and interests managed?
- To what degree are the foreign activities of constituent governments in the federal system competitive and to what degree are they cooperative?

6.2 Twelve Federal Countries—Triangulation Stage

A major task of the theme coordinator was to identify 12 federal countries whose contributions would ensure the theme's adequate exploration from all relevant perspectives.[5] For each of these countries the theme coordinator had further to appoint one or two country coordinators whose task was to choose for each national roundtable 10–20 participants. Because the selection of these participants would have direct impact on the success of the learning process, they had to be chosen according to a given set of criteria. Rather than placing the priority on hierarchical positions, participants were selected to ensure that as far as possible all points of view and all experiences related to the given topic were represented. At least one person had to represent the executive, legislative, and civil service (in particular diplomats) from federal and constituent unit governments.

In addition, it was expected that there would also be members of civil society organizations, business representatives involved in cross-border exports, journalists, scholars, and young professionals. The last were invited to ensure the inclusion of a fresh and out-of-the-box look on the subject. The selection of participants had furthermore to reflect an accurate picture of the political situation in a given country.

6.3 Program Manual—Accommodation Stage

A major challenge of the program was to organize in three months twelve different national and one international roundtable. It is important that these events were held under comparable conditions and that they followed the exact same procedural structure. To be familiar with their tasks, the theme and country coordinators were provided with a manual that outlined in detail the guidelines and responsibilities of running the roundtables and editing the subsequent publications. Much space in the manual was given to the description of the coordinators' role as moderators of the roundtables, as well as to the explanation of the dialogue-oriented communication rules (see subsection 2.2.2). The manual also gave precise instructions on how the roundtable facilities had to be set up, such as, the tables had to be organized in a closed circle,

---

5. The 12 were Argentina, Australia, Austria, Belgium, Canada, Germany, India, Malaysia, South Africa, Spain, Switzerland, and the United States.

with no panel and no electronic appliances. Also, the theme and country coordinators got a small honorarium for their efforts; all other participants were expected to participate with no financial compensation other than a per diem to cover their travel expenses.

6.4 Country Roundtables—Internalization Stage

The national roundtable was a one-day workshop, in most cases, held in the capital of each country between April and June 2006 (see Photos 6–13). In general, the roundtables were held in the major national language.

The cross-cutting questions in the template guided the structure of the roundtables. The aim of the events was to enable participants to reflect on their own experience in light of the contemporary research and theory, as summarized in the theme template. The individual self-reflections conveyed an overall impression of how to position the different countries' policies regarding foreign relations of constituent units in the given knowledge frame.

Shortly after the event, the country coordinators wrote a short article (three pages) that summarized the individual reflections and highlighted the new insights, key issues, and items of international interest that arose at the particular country roundtable. The text had to be written in English in a readable journalistic style so it would be straightforward and accessible for everybody who would want to get an initial impression about the country's stance on foreign relations.

6.5 International Roundtable—Externalization Stage

About three months after the country event, representatives from each roundtable gathered at an international roundtable held in Ottawa, Canada, on October 23 and 24, 2006 (see Photos 14 and 15). The theme coordinator, under the operational auspice of the Forum of Federations, organized and moderated the event, which was held in English. The representatives included the 12 country coordinators, one additional representative from each country roundtable, and selected members of the editorial board, International Association of Centers for Federal Studies, and the Forum of Federations.

Multiyear Global Program Roundtables | 115

Photos 6–13 Global Dialogue Program Country Roundtables

Chicago, USA

Vienna, Austria

Brussels, Belgium

Berlin, Germany

New Delhi, India

Zürich, Switzerland

Brasilia, Brazil

Moscow, Russia

The participants shared their varied experiences and perspectives, as well as the knowledge gained from their country roundtable, to identify commonalities and differences on the theme. The goal of this event was to have individuals become more receptive to innovative ideas and points of view so that they could see and interpret their own country's social and political realities in new ways. The diversity of the countries and internationally generated viewpoints offered participants a broad understanding of the theme, allowing for a truly comparative dialogue.

Following the event in Ottawa, the country coordinators were asked to edit a paper in English that reflected the dialogue of their national roundtable as well as the comparative exchanges of the international roundtable. Each paper was to capture the key issues, areas of consensus, and major disagreements related to the featured theme, using the theme template as a guide to ensure comparability. This comprehensive paper was expected to be an in-depth document that followed scientific standards, which would allow readers to understand the overall subject as well as the content discussed.

Photos 14 and 15   Global Dialogue Program International Roundtable

International Roundtable, Ottawa, Canada. (Left picture, from left to right) Hans Michelmann, Professor, George Anderson, President Forum of Federations, and Former President of Switzerland, Arnold Koller.

6.6 Theme Paper—Reconceptualization Stage

Immediately after the event, the theme coordinator wrote a comparative overview and synthesis based on the content of the international roundtable dialogues and all the written products, including the theme template, the short country roundtable articles, and the comprehensive country papers. The core aims of this theme paper were to derive new patterns and insights and to give a prospective outlook, with new models and trends on how federal countries organize foreign relations carried out by their constituent units. This draft paper was shared with the country coordinators, the editorial board, and the two program host organizations for further suggestions to assure that everybody's perspectives were reflected in the final document.

6.7 Online Discussion Forum—Transformation Stage

In an effort to have a wider audience validate the newly developed knowledge and to launch a dialogue about its application and relevance in other countries, the theme paper was posted in an online discussion forum as part of the Forum of Federations Web site.[6] The forum was structured by concrete questions, where the participants were asked to comment on the practical implications of the new findings in regard to their domestic political context.

6.8 Handbook and Booklet Series— Configuration Stage

To ensure that the knowledge gained at the national and international roundtables did not end with only those who participated in them, all program documents were published (in English) as well as posted on the Forum of Federations online library.[7] The short country roundtable articles were published in a booklet, together with additional educational features such as a map of each country, a glossary, and a list of the program participants (Blindenbacher and Pasma 2007). The purposes of this publication were to make the theme accessible for anybody with an interest in the topic and to provide an entry point to each corresponding handbook. Furthermore, its short length made its translation in multiple languages affordable.[8]

The revised country and theme papers, supplemented with an index, a participant list, and an exhaustive bibliography, underwent a scholarly review process before being published in a handbook (Michelmann

---

6. This online discussion forum was launched after the second program theme and suspended after theme number six.
7. For the Forum of Federations online library see http://www.forumfed.org/en/federalism/library.php.
8. The booklet "Dialogues on Foreign Relations in Federal Countries" is available in Arabic, English, French, German, and Spanish.

2009). This book conveys a profound and updated insight into the topic of foreign relations of constituent units in federal countries. It is intended to be a compendium for practitioners and academics alike. The handbook further describes relevant prospective views about new trends and practices in the field.

The posting of all the program publications on the Web site enabled additional people around the world to become involved in this global dialogue. And thanks to the online discussion forum, the newly developed knowledge got continuously reviewed and updated according to upcoming changes in federal countries worldwide.

6.9 Final Comments and Evaluation

One of the main objectives of the Global Dialogue Program from the very beginning was to stimulate not only learning but also networking among individuals with a common interest in the study and practice of federalism. The participants included almost 250 individuals from 12 countries. To increase the networking opportunities among this core group, all the names and organizational affiliations were listed so anyone—participants or readers—could get in touch whenever they wanted. Furthermore, on a regular basis, these network members received information and updates about the other program themes to interconnect the different program networks with each other. So far this overall network embraces 2,000 core members and is continuously expanding and being strengthened as individuals who get involved with the program themes also get involved in the ongoing online discussion forums.

Theme five of the Global Dialogue Program was very well received in a Level One evaluation conducted with the national and international roundtable participants. In an independently conducted evaluation of the first five themes of the program, theme five was consistently favorably well rated, as were the previous four themes. With respect to *the overall satisfaction*, the combined average score of ratings for the national roundtables was 4.65; for the international roundtable it was 4.77, on a scale of 5. This positive feedback was supported by the qualitative feedback of the evaluation study, which makes it clear that "the overall judgment of the Global Dialogue Program from the perspective of the participants in the roundtables was very favorable" (Meekison 2007). This last conclusion is mirrored in comprehensive feedback from the former President of Switzerland three years after completion of the program portion. He was a participant at the Swiss theme country roundtable as well as at the international roundtable (see Box 3).

> **Box 3 Reflections from the Former President of Switzerland**
>
> As a member of the government of Switzerland, the first step I would take when contending with a political or constitutional problem was to always see how other countries had approached similar issues. Then I could determine how the solution for Switzerland should be tailored. In this light, I have been a great supporter of the Global Dialogue Program. Its approach is designed to develop comparative knowledge about federal countries and good federal practices that are unique in scope, up to date, and cover the practices of federal systems not only as they are written, but as they are implemented. To some extent, participation in the program is like listening to the wisdom of experience that other countries have to offer.
>
> Over the last several years I participated in several national and international Global Dialogue roundtables. Through those experiences I came to the conclusion that what makes the program unique and effective is its comprehensive process; national and international roundtables motivate the participants, who represent diverse viewpoints about a given topic, to share with and learn from each other in a nonpoliticized environment.
>
> Thus, it was with considerable anticipation that I looked forward to participating in the fifth theme of the Global Dialogue Program, that of Foreign Relations in Federal Countries, as it was considered to be a timely topic. As a member of the Swiss government, I faced mounting tensions between the federal government and the constituent units, called Cantons. At the time, Cantons were requesting increasingly a say in foreign policy, especially when their internal powers were concerned.
>
> Foreign policy had traditionally been the responsibility of central governments. However, the scope and nature of constituent unit involvement in Switzerland and in many other federations has grown as the volume of international transactions and the number of international treaties and international organizations has increased dramatically in the last half century. These changes led in turn to ever-growing cross-border relations
>
> *(Box continues on the following page.)*

> **Box 3 (continued)**
>
> and to numerous interferences of the federal governments into the competencies of the constituent units. As a result, constituent units in many countries have become more engaged in international activities because the exercise of their constitutional responsibilities has been increasingly affected by globalization.
>
> This is in particular true for Switzerland, and it was one of the reasons I insisted that in the revision of the federal constitution in 1999 the principle that foreign relations are a federal matter was repeated, but that the Cantons shall participate in the preparation of decisions of foreign policy that concern their powers or their essential interests and that the Cantons may conclude treaties with foreign countries within the scope of their powers.
>
> In this light it was interesting for me to explore with my Swiss colleagues at the Global Dialogue roundtable issues such as: What constitutional powers do the federal governments and constituent states have to conduct foreign affairs? To what degree are relations between orders of government regularized by formal agreements or informal practice? What roles do constituent governments have in negotiating and implementing international treaties? How are international activities and interests managed? To what degree are the foreign activities of constituent governments in the federal system competitive, and to what degree are they cooperative?
>
> As a former Minister of Justice of Switzerland, I was particularly interested in constitutional issues, and I was curious to learn, at the international roundtable, the broad spectrum of how other countries deal with these questions. For example, at one end of the spectrum are Canada and Australia, in which constitutional conventions and court rulings define the terrain and give constituent units significant scope for action. In other countries, including India, Malaysia, and South Africa, the constitution explicitly assigns powers over foreign relations only to the federal government. At the other end of the spectrum are countries whose constitutions assign explicit powers to the constituent units—Argentina, Germany, and Belgium. At our national roundtable we concluded that Switzerland belongs to this latter group and it is important to keep a balance between the participation of the constituent units and the necessary freedom of action of the federal government in foreign policy.

Box 3 (*continued*)

One of my further conclusions was that both orders of government have their particular expertise, and both contribute to the development and maintenance of an effective foreign relations policy. Governments of constituent units on one hand do have a detailed understanding of the cross-border interests and concerns and do have much relevant technical expertise. On the other hand, federal governments do bring greater experience to bear in dealing with the international environment and wield greater political and economic clout than single constituents or groups of constituent units do. Their cooperation requires consultation through durable and adequately conceptualized institutions of intergovernmental relations, and it requires the willingness to make compromises.

In summary, I learned a lot from participating in Global Dialogue roundtables as well as from the publications emanating from the program, and I was not surprised when a recent independent evaluation of the program concluded that the roundtables and the resulting materials are of great value for states that are designing their federal system or struggling with developing new policies, because they get an opportunity to learn how others have resolved similar challenges. It is therefore not surprising that the program has become a useful tool for practitioners and academics alike to acquire a comparative view of a variety of solutions to problems federal governments typically encounter. The program encourages participating practitioners and scholars to use the knowledge they gained to inspire new solutions, thereby improving democratic governance, and to join the many active participants around the world in expanding and strengthening the growing international network on federalism.

Arnold Koller, Appenzell, Switzerland, December 8, 2009

7 Study Tour

In August 2008, the World Bank's Middle East and North Africa Region (funder), the United States Institute of Peace (initiator), the World Bank's Legal Vice Presidency, the World Bank Institute's Parliamentary Strengthening Program, and the Swiss Ministry of Foreign Affairs (host) organized in Switzerland a week-long seminar on the Iraqi judiciary system and the second chamber of parliament. The visiting Iraqi delegation consisted of 13 key members of the Iraq Council of Representatives, most of them members of the Constitutional Review Committee, and 7 of the highest ranking officials of the federal Iraqi and the regional Kurdish judiciary systems.

The study tour was geared around visits to Switzerland's judicial and legislative institutions and meetings with international practitioners from eight countries. The aim of the event was to allow the participants to become familiar with a range of different parliamentarian and judicial systems to develop and redefine concrete recommendations, which they would then present to the Iraqi National Parliament. To illustrate the learning process of the study tour, we single out the judiciary portion of the program and describe it in detail according to the eight stages of the Learning Spiral.

7.1 2005 Iraqi Constitution—Conceptualization Stage

In late 2006 the parliament of Iraq established a Constitutional Review Committee with the mandate to propose a slate of amendments to the 2005 Constitution of Iraq. This special amendment process was intended to make critical changes to the Constitution that would increase support for the political and legal framework among all of Iraq's national communities. Since its inception, the Constitutional Review Committee has made considerable progress in formulating critical amendments that cover an array of fundamental political and legal issues. However, a large number of these issues were still left open and needed special attention. Among them were questions particularly related to the Iraqi judiciary system, such as how the regional and national judiciaries should be effectively structured and coordinated; whether regional courts should hear cases arising from national law, and if so, what the court of last appeal should be; whether courts should have subpoena power in other jurisdictions; whether there should be one set of civil and criminal procedures; whether lawyers should be admitted to practice in all courts; and what the jurisdiction and competencies of each of the federal courts were.

To learn about different judiciary models, which could each answer these questions in various ways, a customized study program was designed and conducted by an organizing team. This team had five staff members who represented the governmental and international institutions that were involved in the event organization. The individual staff members also moderated the different event sessions.

The idea of setting up the event as a study tour was based on the belief that the relevance and impact of the event could be increased significantly through face-to-face exchanges among peers. It also gave the delegates the opportunity to meet their international colleagues in their personal work environment. Thus, they got very real and first-hand testimony about the judicial practice and everyday life in the judiciary systems they visited. This type of learning event also allowed the international practitioners to get involved in the dialogue with the delegates in their search for new solutions about the Iraqi judicial system. Furthermore, it was intended to take the participants away from their daily routines and give them a safe space to debate about different issues and challenges.

7.2 Four Judiciary Systems—Triangulation Stage

In a comprehensive analysis, four judicial models were identified as particularly relevant for the Iraqi context. These models covered the whole spectrum between centralized systems, like the one in India, and decentralized models, such as the one in Switzerland. As examples for intermediate models, the systems from Nigeria and Brazil were selected. Accordingly, the chief justices of Brazil (acting), India (former), Nigeria (former), and Switzerland (acting) were invited to participate in the event (see Photo 16). Furthermore, to learn about the mechanisms of legal and organizational coordination between national and subnational courts, the delegates visited the Federal Ministry of Justice, as well as two different subnational courts in Switzerland.

To ensure the success of the study tour, it was critical that the delegates represent all relevant powers and interest groups in the Iraqi judicial system. Thus it was expected that the newly developed solutions would mirror the different political and legal positions in Iraq and therefore have a real chance to be accepted by the various communities and the parliament. By involving some of the most important stakeholders in the learning process, it was further hoped that once the delegation returned home it would be able to build up political momentum strong enough to allow the envisaged legislative process to be carried out.[1]

Photo 16 Content Triangulation

(From left to right) A. M. Ahmadi, Former Chief Justice of India; Medhat Al Mahmoud, Chief Justice of Iraq; Ellen Gracie Northfleet, Former Chief Justice from Brazil; and Muhammadu Lawal Uwais, Former Chief Justice of Nigeria.

7.3 Study Tour Program—Accommodation Stage

Because the study tour was organized for a hand-picked group of participants, the organizing team involved the Iraqi delegation from the beginning in planning the program. The participants were directly involved in the selection of the questions to be discussed as well as the design of the event procedures, which created an exceptional high sense of ownership among the delegates about the event itself. This close consultation between the organizing team and the participants continued during the event, where the two parties discussed potential changes in the ongoing learning process.

The structure of the study tour followed a given pattern that sequenced the various event parts in a particular manner: Field trips always occurred in the afternoon, so whenever it appeared necessary the dialogue could

---

1. Among the selected participants were the Chair of the Constitutional Review Committee, the Chief Justice of the Federal Supreme Court, the Minister of Justice for the Kurdistan Region, senior judges from the federal and regional judiciaries, the dean of the Baghdad law school, and the president of the Iraqi Bar Association.

extend till after dinner. This measure further allowed the participants to reflect on their experiences of the field trips overnight before sharing them in the next morning's reflection meetings. This pattern of consecutive field trips and reflection meetings was followed by two half-day *transformation* sessions, one in the middle and one at the end of the study tour, as well as an evaluation session at the closure of the event.

To ensure a safe and trustworthy learning environment, high priority was given to the delegate's physical security and privacy during the study tour. Whereas the security issues were taken care of by the Swiss authorities, confidentiality was secured by a strict enforcement of the Chatham House rules by the moderators.[2] The event organizer also made sure that the delegation was protected from any public interference. All sessions were held behind closed doors, and with the exception of a few interviews with selected journalists at the end of the event, no further exposure to the media was allowed. To facilitate the dialogue with external peers, all sessions had simultaneous translation.

7.4 Field Trips—Internalization Stage

A key element of the study tour was the field trips[3] as well as the case presentations about the different national judiciary systems from Brazil, India, Nigeria, and Switzerland (see Photos 17 and 18). In these sessions the presenters were asked first to introduce the delegates to their administrational and/or judicial system, and second, to deliver a preliminary answer to the prepared questions that were sent in by the delegates before the event.

The third part of the meetings was reserved for an extensive dialogue, where critical questions were asked about the presented models as well as their possible implications for the Iraqi judiciary system. In these peer-to-peer exchanges the presenters were encouraged to share their opinions about what they thought works well, as well as what should be improved in their own system. By doing this, they inspired the delegates to follow their example and to think about their own worries and reservations about the status quo of the Iraqi system.

---

2. For the definition of the Chatham House rules, see subsection 5.3.
3. Among the trips were the State Chancellery of the Canton of Berne, the Swiss Federal Supreme Court in Lausanne, and the Cantonal Administrational Court of Geneva.

Photos 17 and 18   Field Trips to Federal and Cantonal Courtstables

(From left to right) The Swiss Federal Supreme Court in Lausanne, and the Cantonal Administrational Court of Geneva.

7.5 Reflection Sessions—Externalization Stage

Following the field trips the delegates met the next morning in reflection sessions (see Photos 19 and 20). The meeting room itself was set up with a closed circle of tables with no podium and no designated sitting order. In this arrangement the moderators facilitated sessions, and the participants exchanged in a first phase their individual reflections about their impressions of the field visit. In a second phase, participants searched for similarities and differences between the presented and the Iraqi system and determined to what extent these foreign models may be relevant for the Iraqi situation.

7.6 Vision of Iraqi Judiciary System— Reconceptualization Stage

As a result of the preceding dialogues with peers and the Supreme Court judges from four different countries, and the discussions among the participants during the reflection sessions, the delegates developed a shared vision for how the Iraqi federal and regional judiciary system may be improved.[4] This growing, common understanding evolved and hardened further in numerous informal conversations; many such conversations

---

4. For a description of this vision, see the personal testimony of the Chief Justice of Iraq in Box 4.

were held during the lengthy bus drives to the field trip locations, which in turn gave these travels a particular didactical purpose.

Photos 19 and 20   Reflection Sessions

Meeting room for reflection sessions. On left, translation booth for simultaneous translations.

7.7   Political Roadmap—Transformation Stage

The emerging vision of how to further develop Iraq's judiciary system became the basis of the answers for many of the questions raised at the beginning of the event. Thus the abstract understanding was made operational and relevant for the current political context in Iraq. This was done in the transformation sessions in the middle and at the end of the event.

In particular, in the second session the participants began setting up concrete roadmaps for how to redirect the political debate back home toward the newly developed vision. There was an emerging expectation that the new ideas about the Iraqi federal and regional judiciary system could find a broader acceptance among the different national communities and could therefore be approved by the Iraqi parliament later.

7.8   CD-ROM—Configuration Stage

All presentations and recorded materials produced during the study tour were collected on a CD-ROM and made available to the participants. The materials were put together with the intention that the delegates would use these reference documents for their political and legislative work to persuade others about the developed vision. This new knowledge became thus the background material for an upcoming learning process, which would consider an extended group of Iraqi politicians and other societal stakeholders who were not involved in the process.

7.9 Final Comments and Evaluation

As documented by a Level One evaluation, the participants received this study tour very well. Ninety percent rated the overall usefulness of the activity and the quality of the event design either as good or very good, and 94 percent considered the moderation excellent. Written feedback from a selected participant, drafted one and a half years after the event, shows that the study tour contributed to a greater consensus and understanding among the delegates about the key aspects on the topic (see Box 4).

Despite the different political affiliations and regional and cultural backgrounds, the participants developed a solid and long-lasting network. With the support of the United States Institute of Peace, this network was able to move the legislative agenda effectively forward toward an expected introduction of a modern and widely accepted new judiciary system in Iraq. It was further noted by the organizers that new collaborations were initiated between individual delegates and their international peers. These collaborations covered a broad range of issues, many of them dealing with very different topics than were discussed during the study tour. In this sense, the newly created national network was expanded to an international set of peer contacts dealing with a variety of topics to improve democratic governance.

The overall positive outcome of the study tour also had a strong and long-lasting impact at the organizing institutions, which committed to continuing their support for Iraq's legal and political development. An example of such collaboration was the organization of another study tour set up in partnership between the World Bank and the Swiss government one year later, which was based on the same organizational procedures.[5]

---

5. The study tour was about the Iraqi Kurdistan's Regional Government Civil Service Reform and was held May 24–30, 2009.

> **Box 4 Reflections from the Chief Justice of the Federal Supreme Court and President of the Higher Judicial Council of Iraq**
>
> We had a pressing interest in examining the experience of the countries that have preceded Iraq in choosing and implementing a federal system as a form of government. How is such a system administered; how does it fulfill its responsibilities; is there a centralized judicial institution that administers the judicial system in all the constituent units, and if so, to what extent, or is the regional judiciary in each state run separately without central supervision?
>
> These questions were going through my mind as I set forth, as the head of the Iraqi judicial delegation, to the roundtable. This event offered the Iraqi delegation a golden opportunity to obtain answers to the aforementioned queries through detailed discussions with eminent Swiss politicians, civil servants, and judges from the cantonal (state) and federal level, scholars, as well as three Supreme Court chief justices from Brazil, India, and Nigeria.
>
> We learned in particular about how the Swiss judiciary fulfills its duties in the pursuit of justice and guarantees private and public rights. We visited the courts of several cantons, where we were informed about the laws being applied, particularly the penal and civil procedures as well as the evidence act. We noted there are some differences between the cantons because of differences in culture, traditions, and history, but we also noted a partial or full similarity with regard to certain laws. During our discussions, we found out that there was a shared desire to unify the laws of civil and penal procedures and the evidence act in the federal judicial system and that efforts were being made in this regard.
>
> We realized that although there are some common rules for selecting and promoting judges, some disparities remain in other facets of the judicial systems in the cantons, because of traditions and heritage and the extent of people's attachment to them, as well as the fear of change, which is usually associated with transitional periods. We also examined the role of the federal Supreme Court and its jurisdiction within the federal judicial system. What we found suggests that there is a means to unify jurisprudence and deal with certain rulings issued by the regional judiciary.
>
> I became aware of obvious differences between the Swiss, Brazilian, Indian, and Nigerian judicial systems. These differences can be attributed to several factors, such as the judicial systems of the constituent units, as well as politi-

Box 4 (*continued*)

cal viewpoints or theories in a country, the concept of the federal state, and the jurisdiction of the central authority and the regions, which may vary.

During the roundtable I also reviewed the judicial system in Iraq, which in 2003 adopted a federal political system of government, and examined the repercussions of this new political system on the judicial organization, as well as the future perspectives of the judiciary in Iraq. It is well known that before 2003 the judiciary in Iraq was centrally administered by the Ministry of Justice through a Council of Justice. The Council was presided over by the Minister of Justice, who, of course, was part of the executive authority, which continuously tried to interfere with the independence of the judicial decisions. Following the political changes, the Higher Judicial Council was formed and entrusted with the task of administering the judiciary independently of the Ministry of Justice. The judiciary was then recognized as an independent power, as are the legislative and executive powers.

So what would the role of the federal judiciary be with respect to the regional judiciaries that were formed in accordance with the 2005 Iraqi constitution? Will the regional judiciary remain completely independent from the federal judiciary, and will it continue to be administered autonomously as an independent regional judicial authority, with no supervision whatsoever from the federal judiciary? And if the federal judiciary were to supervise the judiciary in the provinces, what form would such supervision take, and what would be its extent?

After examining the experience of the judiciaries of the Swiss, Brazilian, Indian, and Nigerian federations, I can say that we can benefit from these experiences and use some of their rules when forming the federal and regional judiciary in Iraq. Basically, there will be a judicial authority in each region, which will administer all fields of the region's judiciary, including all matters pertaining to the judges and to the safeguarding of their independence. The federal and regional judiciary shall complement each other and coordinate their work through the membership of the regional judicial authorities' presidents in the Higher Judicial Council. They will draw up the judicial policy in the federal states, set the rules that will guarantee the independence of the judiciary, unify the judicial code of conduct and the rules governing the appointment of judges, ensure compliance with the provisions of the constitution and with the international standards stipulated in international charters and treaties, unify the laws of procedure and

(Box continues on the following page.)

> **Box 4 (*continued*)**
>
> the evidence acts in both the civil and penal field, form federal courts in the regions that would dispose of disputes arising from the federal government's exercise of its exclusive powers or other powers stipulated by the constitution and by federal laws, and form regional courts to dispose of disputes arising from the regional governments' exercise of their non-exclusive powers.
>
> This is a summary of our vision of the federal and regional judiciary in Iraq based on the actual Iraqi situation and our examination made during the roundtable.
>
> Medhat Al Mahmoud, Baghdad, Iraq, May 4, 2009

8 Evaluation-Based Workshop

The Independent Evaluation Group (IEG) has the mandate of assessing the development effectiveness of World Bank support and is a unit within the World Bank structure, reporting directly to the Board of Executive Directors. One of IEG's core assignments is to disseminate its report findings in all sorts of outreach and learning activities.

In 2008 IEG completed the last of a series of four comprehensive evaluation reports related to the same overarching topic of public sector reform. Based on particularly high interest in the topic, IEG organized—in collaboration with the World Bank Office in Ethiopia, the Africa Region's Public Sector Reform and Capacity Building Unit,[1] the Public Sector Governance Group,[2] and the World Bank Institute[3]—an evaluation-based learning event. This event was held in Addis Ababa, Ethiopia, December 9–10, 2008. The workshop title was "Lessons of a Decade of Public Sector Reform: Voices of African Client Stakeholders." The event was funded by the Norwegian Agency for Development Cooperation (Norad). The invited participants were 60 individuals from 8 African countries, as well as several development partners and regional organization representatives.

The workshop objective was to improve learning among participants who were involved in public sector reform projects and to enhance aid effectiveness in the sector, specifically for donor-supported reforms. This evaluation-based learning approach was structured along the concept of the Learning Spiral, which determined the design of the event. From a World Bank perspective, the workshop aimed to close the feedback loop of the World Bank's activity

---

1. The Africa Region's Public Sector Reform and Capacity Building Unit helps shape the Bank's strategic thinking and operational planning on public sector governance and reform in client countries in the Sub-Sahara Africa Region.
2. The Public Sector Governance Group brings together people working across the Bank on lending and nonlending activities that relate to core public sector reform.
3. The World Bank Institute is the learning and capacity building unit of the World Bank.

cycle, where projects are executed by operations and then evaluated by IEG, which in turn disseminates its findings as lessons learned to the sectors, operations, The World Bank Institute, and client countries.

8.1 Four Evaluation Reports—Conceptualization Stage

Improving public sector effectiveness and efficiency is a priority item on the reform agenda of most African countries. In setting up a learning event, IEG considered four evaluation reports closely related to the topic that had been published between 2005 and 2008.[4] The specific content of the reports dealt with decentralization, financial accountability assessments, procurement assessment, and capacity building in Africa. To make the four evaluation reports readily accessible, they were summarized and the summary given to the workshop participants a few weeks prior to the workshop. The content of the summary was further condensed into two basic and interrelated lessons, which gave the workshop its distinctive content structure: In the first half of the workshop, the lesson discussed was that effective public sector reform has to be based on a coherent and country-owned strategy. In the second half, the given lesson dealt with was that appropriate capacities that allow the implementation of these strategies have to be systematically strengthened.

In addition to the written documents, and to make sure that every participant had the same level of information, at the opening session of the workshop two IEG staff members introduced the key findings and the lessons learned. This gave the participants an early opportunity to comment and to validate the presented findings. This measure allowed IEG to complement and update the evaluation results and allowed the participants to find initial common ground.

To ensure the ownership of the workshop by the involved World Bank units, each unit delegated one staff member to the organizing team who would be responsible for all operational and procedural tasks related to the event. The team was led by one of the four IEG report authors. With

---

4. The IEG reports included were *Decentralization in Client Countries: An Evaluation of World Bank Support, 1997–2007* (2007b); *Public Sector Reform: What Works and Why?* (2008b); *Country Financial Accountability Assessments and Country Procurement Assessment Reports: How Effective Are World Bank Fiduciary Diagnostics?* (2008c); and *Capacity Building in Africa* (2005) (see http://www.worldbank.org/ieg/).

the exception of the team leader, all other team members acted as moderators of either the plenary sessions or the breakout groups.

8.2 Eight African Countries—Triangulation Stage

Most participants at the workshop were selected from eight African countries, including the five Anglophone countries of Ethiopia (host), Nigeria, Sierra Leone, Sudan, and Tanzania, and the three Francophone countries of the Democratic Republic of Congo, Madagascar, and Rwanda. About five participants represented each country; they had been selected based on their involvement in designing and implementing public sector reform projects. To take into account the complexity of public sector reform in multilevel governmental systems and to ensure that the relevant perspectives were considered, the invited participants represented all major spheres in the national and subnational levels, as well as policy makers and civil servants. In addition, each delegation included at least one participant from a nongovernmental organization.

The actual appointment of the selected individuals was made in collaboration with the World Bank country offices and the selected governments. To enrich the range of perspectives, other experts and practitioners were invited, such as two international experts from South Africa and South Korea; several representatives of development partners, including the African Development Bank, the Danish International Development Assistance, the European Union, and the German Technical Cooperation; and representatives from regional organizations such as the African Union, the Pan-African Conference of Ministers for Public Service, and the African Training and Research Center for Administration in Development. To round out the perspectives, the conference organizers were also represented at the workshop by at least one participant. In all, there were close to 60 participants at the event.

8.3 Concept Note and Guidance Note— Accommodation Stage

To make the learning process transparent and accessible, a concept note was prepared to describe the purpose, objectives, and structure of the workshop. The overarching message in this document was that all participants would have equal treatment during the workshop. This measure was particularly challenging because the hierarchical differences among the participants were wide; participants ranged from lower-level governmental advisors up to the Prime Minister of Ethiopia (see Photo 21). All participants were seated around a closed rectangle, with no podium (see Photo 23). To ease the communication between the French- and English- speaking participants, the dialogue in the plenary sessions had simultaneous translation.

In an additional guidance note, the methodologies of the workshop as well as the specific roles of the different participants were explained. Strong emphasis was given to the description of the communication rules, which bound all participants equally. Among them were the Chatham House Rules, which regulate the exchange of information with the outside world.[5] Other rules were applied to the regulation of the formal exchange, such as five-minute speaking time limits and the prohibition of PowerPoint® presentations.

Two moderators enforced the communication rules in the plenary sessions. They were members of the organizing team and were selected based on their political impartiality; neither of them was involved in the public sector reform projects discussed and neither had any authorship in the reports. The design of the workshop required that one actively facilitate the dialogue and the other observe the process dynamics and ensure that all participants had an equal amount of time to speak. The two handled this task as a team and rotated their roles after each session. Because there was and no *head* of the table, they were, despite their distinct role, integrated in the same seating order as everyone else (see Photo 22).

Photo 21 Seating in Plenary Session

(From right to left) Meles Zenawi, Prime Minister of Ethiopia; Kenichi Ohashi, World Bank Country Director to Ethiopia; and Anand Rajaram, World Bank Regional Manager, Sub-Saharan and North African Region.

---

5. For the definition of the Chatham House rules, see subsection 5.3.

Each participant received a large package of documents prior to the event beginning, including a personal invitation letter, the workshop agenda, the concept and guidance notes, the IEG evaluation summary, and a fact sheet from the World Bank country offices. To remind the participants about the main principles of the workshop, the two moderators gave a short presentation about the workshop proceedings at the workshop inauguration.

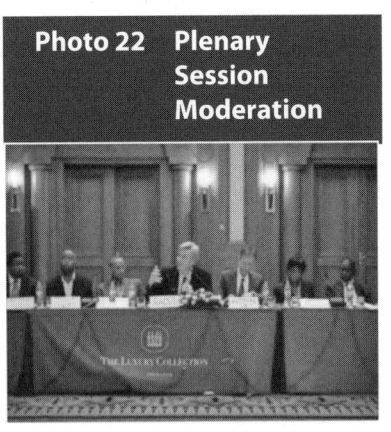

Photo 22 Plenary Session Moderation

The two moderators of the plenary sessions (fourth and fifth from left).

8.4 Plenary Sessions—Internalization Stage

At the center of the workshop were two identically structured half-day sessions. Each focused on one of the two main lessons. In the first part of the session, the plenary session (see Photo 23), three participants reflected in a short statement on the lesson at stake in light of their respective country experience.

The three speakers were chosen from different countries and held different positions; this ensured the diversity of perspectives. The statements were informal in style and reflected the personal opinion of the speaker. This is unlike formal governmental conference settings, where official positions are presented from prepared texts.

These statements were structured along several key guiding questions, which were directed to each of the lessons. Among the questions raised for the first session were How could participants motivate public sector reform? How could they generate ownership? And how could they use international experience? For the

Photo 23 Plenary Session

Roundtable with 60 participants.

second session the questions were How did participants understand capacity development challenges? How could stakeholders' views be integrated? And how should capacity development activities be prioritized?

The presentations were followed by statements from the rest of the participants, who also described their individual experiences. The session closed with a short commentary by the international experts, who presented their experiences from a global viewpoint. These added further perspectives to the table.

8.5 Breakout Groups—Externalization Stage

To share the reflections made in the previous stage—the Internalization Stage—in the second part of the workshop session, the plenary split into two parallel breakout groups. These groups were moderated by two other members of the organizing team to give the two plenary session moderators the freedom to follow the process in both groups and thus get a continuous overview of the overall workshop progress.

Photo 24   Breakout Group

Breakout group with the representatives of the Francophone countries.

The purpose of the breakout groups was to create a more intimate space that would allow participants to share their individual reflections from the previous plenary session among their peers. The groups were formed along French- and English-speaking participants to ease communication and obviate the need for simultaneous translation (see Photo 24).

Based on the shared country experiences in the plenary session, the emphasis in the breakout groups was on developing new insights and practices around effective and country-owned public sector reform strategies and about effective capacity building.

8.6 Review of Evaluation Reports—Reconceptualization Stage

In the first part of the final workshop session, the breakout group facilitators reported their observations to the plenary about new patterns and insights raised in the two groups with regard to country-owned public sector reform strategies and capacity building. These observations were complemented by the individual lessons learned that one country and three donor representatives shared. In the ensuing dialogue, a modified understanding of effective public sector reform projects was adopted. By operating this way, the original results of the evaluation findings became redefined and updated to fit the latest course of action.

8.7 Action Plan—Transformation Stage

The purpose of the final plenary session was to discuss the impact of the new findings on future public sector reform projects. For this purpose the workshop participants drafted, under the guidance of the moderators, an action plan under which all participants committed themselves to taking concrete measures and to applying their new insights to their particular frame of action (see Photo 25). This process also included the participation of the World Bank staff, who committed themselves to supporting the implementation of the country-specific action plans.

Photo 25 Action Planning

The workshop team leader (second from left) working on the action plan developed in real time by the workshop participants.

8.8 Brochure—Configuration Stage

For the purpose of configuring the newly reframed knowledge and its contextual application, the workshop results, including the different action plans, were summarized in *Lessons of a Decade of Public Sector Reform: Voices of African Client Stakeholders* (IEG 2008e). The document reflects all relevant information about the event in an easily accessible and readable manner. It can be understood as an extension of and the actualization of the existing evaluation reports and was added as appendix to the four report Web sites. Furthermore, the findings were publicly disseminated at a press conference and through numerous interviews organized by IEG, with the participation of prominent workshop participants.

8.9 Final Comments and Evaluation

The different action plans developed in the transformation stage triggered a whole range of bilateral and multilateral follow-up activities, many of them directly supported by diverse World Bank units (IEG 2008e). Through this process, a number of small networks were created among countries committed to working together on particular subjects in public sector reform.

A further important product of the event was the brochure about the workshop results, which updated and complemented the existing four IEG evaluation reports from the perspective of eight African countries (IEG 2008e). This new knowledge was subsequently integrated into IEG's dissemination process, that is, in a learning event about public sector reform, organized by the World Bank's Middle East and North African Region unit immediately after the workshop. In a figurative way, this follow-up event is an example how a next new spin of the learning spiral is set in motion.

The workshop was reviewed by the participants in a Level One evaluation conducted at the end of the workshop. The results were remarkable because the average ratings were segmented according to the different participant groups: in a scale of 1 (very bad) to 5 (very good), the representatives from governments rated the *relevance of the workshop to the current work* the highest (4.8), followed by the nonprofit organizations (4.7) and the donor organizations (4.3). The average rating was 4.56.

In regard to the *overall usefulness of the activity*, members of governments rated the event 4.8, nonprofit organizations rated it 4.7, and donor organizations rated it 3.9. The average rating was 4.45. The workshop had also some long-term impact, as is seen in a feedback letter from an individual participant of the Ethiopian government more than one year after the event (see Box 5).

Box 5 Reflections from the Director of Planning and Programming Directorate, Ministry of Capacity Building of the Government of Ethiopia

I participated in the workshop as a team member of the delegation of the Ethiopian government. As head of Planning and Programming Directorate of the federal Ministry of Capacity Building in Ethiopia, I am very much engaged in the implementation of public sector reform and capacity building initiatives already under way in the country in various sectors at different tiers of government.

How the Ethiopian government embarked on the public sector reform and capacity building programs is best described with historical trajectories. The incumbent government came to power by overthrowing the former socialist military regime with armed struggle. This coincided with the end of the Cold War, economic governance reform toward a market economy, multiparty democratization ideology, glocalization (globalization and localization at the same time)—all happened worldwide in developed and developing countries alike. The Ethiopian government, with a new constitution, introduced federal arrangements mainly based on national identity/ethnicity, multiparty democracy, market economy, and decentralization and launched these almost at the same time in the early and mid-1990s. The underpinning principles of the current Ethiopian government policies are referred to as a mix of market economy, revolutionary democracy, and developmental state. These underpinning principles are considered basics for other government policies and strategies. Strategies were prepared by the Ethiopian government for rural and agricultural development, industrial and infrastructural development, and social development starting around the end of last decade. Capacity building and public sector reform programs were designed roughly at the same time to assist the effective implementation of these sectoral strategies. These reform programs have been under implementation for about a decade and a lot of stories can be told of their successes and challenges.

As a person closely engaged in this process for five or so years, I had various questions in mind, and of course many of them were recurring on different occasions at meetings with stakeholders. Some questions relate to political ownership and commitment; governance structure for leading,

(Box continues on the following page.)

> **Box 5 (*continued*)**
>
> coordinating, and managing public sector reform and capacity building initiatives; management of public sector reform in decentralized/federal systems where subnational governments maintain certain sovereignty; the role of institutional and human resources capacity to implement the reform; and the role of development partners. There are also basic questions related to the political economy of public sector reform: public sector reform for what (demand, purpose), who (drivers, targets), how (effective strategy), and when (timing, sequencing, sustainability).
>
> The workshop was helpful in shedding light on questions like these by providing the opportunity to discuss experiences of other countries in Africa. Resource allocation from own source, committed governance structure to play a leadership role, and supporting rules and regulations are considered indicative of political ownership and commitment to the reform in a country. It was also emphasized during the workshop that institutional and human resources capacity plays a key role in the implementation of public sector reform. Participants in the workshop reiterated the need for deploying and retaining the requisite human resources in order to be able to effectively implement the reform. It was observed that even when the political ownership seems to be high, institutional and human resource capacity remain challenging in many African countries. This is what I feel is relevant here in Ethiopia as well.
>
> Regarding the leadership and coordination structure of the reform, the participants took note of various possibilities that depended on the contextual environment. The Ethiopian government has organized a separate ministry in charge of initiating, leading, and coordinating the management of public sector reform. In Tanzania, a coordinating body was set up in the president's office, and the steering committee established for this purpose makes sure implementation and coordination of the reform in various sectoral ministries and agencies go smoothly. In Nigeria, state governments are said to be autonomous and normally are left to their own discretion. Development partners were expected to directly engage themselves with state governments in supporting the public sector reform initiatives in Nigeria.
>
> Another learning point relates to the role of development partners. It was recommended that the World Bank and other development partners remain engaged with countries even when the political ownership and

Box 5 (*continued*)

commitment are lacking. The consensus by the participants was that the World Bank role needs to be leading with creative ideas and best practices, particularly through technical support instead of dictating to governments using its financial power. I found this understanding very important in our case, as it provides an opportunity to maintain an engaged dialogue with development partners including the World Bank.

I feel the most important impact of the workshop has to do with the confidence it gave me in my role as a professional staff dealing with public sector reform in day-to-day operations. The experiences, success factors, and challenges I learned about during the workshop have given me the impetus to play a much larger role in the country's public sector reform agenda.

Finally, I must say that I was very much impressed by the management of the workshop process, where an enormous number of lessons and future actions were covered only within the two days of the workshop. The workshop discussions and resulting materials will remain valuable for me and other practitioners of public sector reform in the Ethiopian government.

Ato Ahmed Mohammed Ali, Addis Ababa, Ethiopia, January 12, 2010

9 Multimedia Training and E-Learning Initiative

MP3IC is a global multimedia training and e-learning initiative spearheaded by the World Bank Institute (WBI), the Asian Development Bank Institute (ADBI), and the Multilateral Investment Fund of the Inter-American Development Bank (IADB). Its goal is to promote capacity building and knowledge sharing among practitioners, researchers, and development agencies around the world in the area of private-public partnership (PPP) infrastructure projects. The program's ambition is to use cutting-edge pedagogy and multimedia technology to transform existing research findings and practice into user-friendly messages that developing country public sector professionals can use in their day-to-day problem solving.

Considering the global scope of the learning initiative, the MP3IC core organizing team represents an international consortium representing WBI, ADBI, and IADB. The team is extended through core partners, involving leading national public sector training institutions in governmental capacity building around the world. The target audiences of the program are public sector leaders and senior officials from all levels of government, as well as other leaders who represent the private sector and civil society from all over the world. This rather selective choice of learning actors allows maximal reach and impact on efforts to achieve effective and efficient public service delivery in a short period.

To develop the specific training and e-learning considerations that need to be taken into account when designing the program's concept and its different core learning components (CLCs), ADBI—in close collaboration with WBI and the Development Academy of the Philippines (host)—organized a symposium, "Strengthening Governance for Infrastructure Service Delivery: The Role of Public Private Partnerships." It was held March 9–11, 2009, at ADB headquarters in Manila. The symposium brought together important stakeholders for governance capacity building—more than 40 leading global and regional governance experts and senior-level managers of leading public sector training institutes from 13 countries across the Asia-Pacific region.

The objective of the event was to profile and share pragmatic governance learning materials and didactic concepts that facilitate designing of CLCs and to enable the participating training institutions to strengthen their learning on governance capacity building. In this context, the Learning Spiral was introduced and discussed as the foundation on which the MP3IC program, as well as its global multimedia training and learning segment, the CLCs, would be structured.[1] The following description of the eight stages of the Spiral presents the outcome of this dialogue and describes in detail how the Learning Spiral should be applied to ensure the program's effectiveness.

The MP3IC Program considered this 2009 event as the basis for planning the design and use of CLCs. As of publication, this planning is still in development.

9.1 Core Learning Components— Conceptualization Stage

The training and learning content of the MP3IC initiative consists of a comprehensive set of 54 topics representing the major themes in PPPs in infrastructure capacity building. They were selected by the MP3IC team in consultation with the partner organizations. It is foreseen that each of the topics will be broadly covered in a CLC module, which consists— among other things—of two main parts:

1. The concrete and measurable training and e-learning objectives, which are based on generic content goals (accountability goals). This helps the learning actors retain the basic knowledge and objectives to be measured, which in turn allows them to apply the acquired knowledge to their individual political environments (learning goals).

2. The content of the CLCs, which is processed and edited by leading experts in the field and subsequently reviewed by focus groups and

---

[1]. The Learning Spiral was presented by the author in a keynote speech: http://www.adbi.org/speeches/2009/07/13/3173.keynote.speech.blindenbacher.pppi.governance/.

expert panels in regard to their relevance for the target audience. This measure is essential because the understanding of PPPs in infrastructure and related topics is globally very controversial; a common understanding of the subject has first to be established.

To make the CLCs accessible and attractive to a global audience, the collected knowledge has to be packed into a set of various data carriers, including print products and self-sustaining media presentations such as audio and video clips. It further has to be complemented by a glossary that explains the specific terminology used in the CLCs. In addition, it should be translated into as many languages as the target audience needs. For this purpose, an Internet portal designed particularly for the MP3IC initiative can be established that will allow the storage of a great deal of data and knowledge as well as their exchange among a specified target audience. It will be important to keep resources and information on the portal up to date to stay relevant for its users and to create incentives for them to return to the portal periodically. The portal needs to integrate user-friendly features from existing networks and platforms to make it intuitive and attractive to site visitors.

9.2 Global Target Audience—Triangulation Stage

To increase the attractiveness and relevance of the material for a broad target audience, the program partners must identify the major existing perspectives in regard to the content of the CLCs. In the case of PPPs in infrastructure, the perspectives are exceptionally diverse. On the public sector side they include politicians and members of Parliament from all different levels of government, judges from national and subnational courts, representatives of political parties, the civil service, and members of state-owned entities. On the private sector side, there are business leaders, investors, lenders, members of business associations and consortia, and lobbying organizations. And finally on the civil society side, there are the stakeholders representing not-for-profit organizations, the media, think tanks, scholars of different academic disciplines, and members of organized communities and networks that communicate through blogs and other information technology–supported means.

For each perspective, a representative stakeholder has to be chosen to describe his or her personal viewpoint concerning the issue at stake. This should preferably be done in the form of short narratives illustrated by concrete cases based on the authors' real-world experiences; the learning actors should be able to easily relate to them. Each story can be captured both in a traditional paper-based format and in a more interactive video format. This supplement essentially mirrors the content of the CLCs by putting the key takeaways of the learning material into multiple perspectives. This exhaustive set of material includes the state-of-the-art knowledge on each topic as well as the narrative supplements.

The combination of the range of topics, their broad treatment, and their nonhierarchical organization in modules and submodules with different content focus and depth is designed to get the attention and curiosity of the target audience and to serve their diverse needs and expectations. It will allow the learning actors to navigate through the wide range of modules and to choose specific CLCs according to their personal needs and interests.

9.3 Users' Manual—Accommodation Stage

Crucial for such a multimedia training and e-learning initiative are personal contacts among the learning actors and the organizing MP3IC team—at the earliest possible stage in the process. Ideally, the inauguration of the program would be a face-to-face event involving all potential participants. If such an event were not possible, a number of regional or national events, a multiscreen videoconference, or a combination of them could substitute. The purpose of such an event is to ensure that the participants get to know each other and have an opportunity to build trust and confidentiality among themselves and the organizers. These newly established personal relationships also ease future written communication as well as individual phone or video encounters.

At the same time, the MP3IC portal needs to foster networking opportunities among the participants by providing sophisticated but simple-to-use spaces to build user profiles and connect with each other. These profiles would include a user's picture, professional affiliation, interests and hobbies, and organizational affiliation. It will be important for users to be able to send each other private messages through such platforms and to be able update other participants about their latest work, initiatives they joined or support, and causes they promote. Such a space would combine the philosophies used by social media such as Facebook® and LinkedIn® to connect people with similar interests and professional affiliations, while making the platform very easy to use.

Preceding these first contacts, the organizers have to ensure that the participants are fully aware of the philosophy and the structure of the learning process, its objectives, and the communication and privacy rules. This last element determines how the participants are supposed to communicate with each other. Furthermore, it suggests how to handle cultural and regional differences. All this program-related information has to be summarized in a sourcebook or a user's manual, which would be made available to all potential learning actors in a printed publication; it can also be posted on the MP3IC portal.

Because many of the interpersonal and group interactions will be made through the electronic MP3IC portal, technical support and security systems play a crucial role. Appropriate protection programs and firewalls have to be installed and a helpdesk set in place to deliver technical support to all participants at any time.

9.4 Online Questionnaire—Internalization Stage

In a first didactical step, the participants get an opportunity to reflect on their own practices in light of the knowledge to be learned in the content of the 54 recorded CLCs. This intrapersonal activity can be encouraged by posting a set of targeted questions about the subject that make people think about and reveal their personal experiences; this triggers the intended self-reflection process. To ensure that the learning actors understand the content of the CLCs, it may be further envisaged that an assessment instrument could be installed at the MP3IC portal, such as a readiness scorecard that would allow the participants to self-assess their understanding of the knowledge to be learned.

Additionally, the MP3IC portal needs to include an elaborate library of resources—not already part of the CLC content—so the participants can find materials on the subject matter. Such materials could include a broad spectrum of resources such as books, articles, case studies, reports, white papers, video clips, etc. Compilation of resources in a library will allow easy and organized access to critical knowledge and can provide a strong and common reference point.

The MP3IC portal may also include a private online account, in which the learning actors are asked to store notes about their individual learning experiences. This private account could only be accessed by its designated owner and would be secured with a personal password. However, if the account owner wished to do so, he or she should have the freedom to give access to other individuals. This measure protects the account holder's privacy, prevents any loss of written materials, and regulates the process of sharing these personal notes with peers.

9.5 Online Dialogue Exchange—Externalization

In the second didactical step, the learning actors are encouraged to engage with the other participants in an active dialogue to share their individual reflections. This dialogue can be held in blogs or discussion forums installed at the MP3IC portal or though social networking platforms such as Facebook®, Ning®, and WordPress®, where selected individuals are invited to communicate in groups in a protected and private online environment.

This highly sensitive and confidential online dialogue exchange has to be well facilitated and closely supervised by members of the MP3IC team. It is their responsibility to enforce the given communication rules, to structure the dialogue, and to ensure that all participants have the same chance to get involved. The MP3IC team will predetermine questions and topics for discussions and ensure the flow of discussions. It will need to send out email invitations to the participants to join the discussions, prepare initial comments to kick-start the discussion, respond to some questions from the participants, and, when needed, redirect the conversation to the relevant topic. It further will have to observe the discussions and ensure that all the questions and comments receive appropriate responses, as well as summarizing the discussions into a document that can be circulated among the participants and, if they agree, among wider audiences of interested practitioners. The preparatory stage may also require the MP3IC team to find and collaborate with a group of seasoned experts on a subject in advance to ensure that they can help create initial comments in the discussions and provide their expert responses along the way.[2]

At the same time, the MP3IC portal can provide a platform for participants to share their documents with each other. Such sharing can help participants get input from their colleagues on their work in progress, such as research papers or studies, and bring a new perspective to the ongoing research. To enable such document sharing, the portal can utilize Google Documents or any other document collaboration technology.

The MP3IC portal will include several features that allow participants to stay updated on the latest activities in the network and recent postings. Along with email updates, it will be important to have an option for a weekly digest and rich site summary (RSS) feeds. The blog and resources on the MP3IC platform can have an option for an RSS feed or instantaneous email update. The RSS feed allows participants to easily track newly posted resources and use them quickly.

Over time these online dialogue exchanges could be transformed into long-lasting communities of practice. These self-organized and theme-oriented peer-to-peer learning groups give participants the opportunity to continuously share their reflections in an institutionalized frame to improve their skills on a given subject, to share information and knowledge with each other, and to create documents that include a wide range of perspectives (see subsection 2.2.3). It will be critical to ensure that members of the community benefit from being part of it. Some incentives to join include substantive knowledge gain and learning opportunities, the ability to showcase expertise for networking purposes, the ability to find peer reviewers and research collaborators, as well as the ability to tap into local knowledge.

To sustain and strengthen a community of practice, it will be important to have face-to-face meetings with the participants. Such meetings both serve as an incentive for more active participation in the externalization of knowledge and can be a catalyst for innovative ideas. It is an established practice that when a group of people are given an appropriate

---

2. This usually requires cultivating long-lasting relationships with various experts and involving them in other types of network activities as a reward for their time. Such activities could be access to training and knowledge, consulting opportunities, publishing their works online, etc.

time and space to brainstorm and find solutions, they are more inclined to think innovatively and suggest different approaches. For this to happen, the MP3IC team needs to ensure the participants that the provided forum is safe for any kind of discussion and suggestion and that everyone is open to new ideas.

9.6 Process Monitoring—Reconceptualization Stage

A major task of the MP3IC team is to watch systematically the ongoing group-reflection process and to monitor the relevance of the CLCs for the current practice in PPP infrastructure projects. If the collective reflections consistently deviate in form and substance from the state-of-the-art knowledge as presented in the CLCs, it is the team members' responsibility, in collaboration with their core partners, to update and if necessary to fully replace their content accordingly. This measure ensures that the content in the MP3IC program always represents the latest knowledge, and it further conveys to the participants a sense that the knowledge they are learning represents the best practices available to date.

One way of encouraging continuous feedback and suggestions from participants on the shared knowledge resources would be to enable the rating of resources. Many Web platforms allow users to rate their content, which provides the site managers with data on user preferences and most used types of materials.

It will also be important to use social networking tools on resources such as Digg®, StumbleUpon®, or de.li.cio.us®. These online tools allow users worldwide not only to bookmark their favorite resources and postings, but also to share them with other users interested in the same subject matter and to share their bookmarks. These tools can be used both to promote resources and knowledge outside the selected group of people and to measure the popularity of resources most bookmarked.

9.7 Scenario Exercises and Rapid Results Approach—Transformation Stage

To get used to the CLC content and to learn how to employ it, the program offers in a third didactical step a guided role-play or scenario exercises. These integrated games allow the learning actors to simulate their individual work situations in light of the new knowledge. The participants are placed in a project situation in which they have to make appropriate decisions that require an in-depth understanding of the CLC substance. In this way the participants become familiar with the knowledge and automatically prepare themselves to apply it into their real work context.

Based on the experiences in the simulation games, in the fourth step the learning actors are asked to develop concrete plans for how they want to integrate the newly acquired knowledge into their own practical field of action. This process can be facilitated by the application of the Rapid Results Approach, which is a management tool that empowers teams to develop 100-day plans that build capacity for large-scale change.[3] With this methodology the learning actors are in a position to develop realistic plans for how to implement the CLC content; they set short-term goals to solidify and accelerate the overall implementation process in a given infrastructure project.

To ensure the success of such a planning process, the regional help desks must work with the local core partner organizations, which are familiar with the specific circumstances the learning actors face. These help desks are expected to give instant assistance whenever the participants request it. An electronic blackboard installed at the MP3IC portal may further support this effort, where participants post questions about the planning process and others respond according to their own experiences. It is important that the participants continuously document and reflect on this process in their electronic journals. Another possibility to gather feedback from the participants is to use surveys on specific issues and quick polls to identify interest in discussion topics, CLC events, etc.

The experience of seeking input from colleagues in the region or around the world can be further maximized when the MP3IC team gathers the responses on the posted questions from various participants or, if needed, even personally contacts selected participants to solicit

---

3. The Rapid Results Approach is a modified version of General Electric's work-out process, first developed in the late 1980s to reduce bureaucracy and redundancy. Over time, its application has broadened to address business processes and to accelerate organizational change (Schaffer and Ashkenas 2005).

responses. Once the responses are collected, supplemental research and literature review on the subject matter could be combined with the participant responses in a consolidated response.

9.8 Revision of CLCs—Configuration Stage

By conducting the multimedia training and e-learning initiative as described so far, a considerable amount of new knowledge related to PPPs in infrastructure capacity building will be developed and electronically loaded at the MP3IC portal. All these data have to be configured to update the CLCs; they also will be summarized in a form that allows their availability for a global audience. For that purpose the learning actors first screen their electronic journals to decide which parts they want to open to the public. The gathered knowledge, complemented by the reviewed and updated CLCs, forms the basis of the most updated and practice-relevant knowledge that exists on the subject.

Second, the core team and partner organizations must integrate this newly developed knowledge into the existing CLCs and summarize it in various media to make it attractive and easily accessible. The purpose of the latter effort is to attract a broad international audience to the MP3IC program and by doing so to expand and strengthen the emerging global network that derives from this initiative. The dissemination of the knowledge is done through the MP3IC portal as well as by all other existing means of communication transfer.

9.9 Final Comments and Evaluation

Multimedia training or e-learning has become one of the major means of supporting learning in governments in recent years, and it is expected that this trend will further accelerate with any forthcoming technological innovation. Also conference Web sites, online discussion forums, etc. were didactical elements used in Learning Spiral–based events in the past.

The MP3IC multimedia training and e-learning initiative is the first program that was systematically geared around social media technologies. It represents a new area of using such instruments to improve the Learning Spiral's impact. Thanks to the targeted application of social media, the dynamism and the intensity of the learning process over time and space can be significantly increased. However, it is important to give high attention to issues such as privacy protection and property rights to avoid jeopardizing the learning actors' confidence in the learning activity as a whole.

It is not fully clear yet how the MP3IC initiative will further develop. Its progress was discussed in a follow-up symposium.[4] Testimony by a leading member of the MP3IC core team describes the relevance of the Learning Spiral concept not only for designing the program but also for its impact on the program development process itself, which is very much organized as a learning activity in its own right (see Box 6).

> **Box 6 Reflections from the Lead Economist, Public-Private Partnerships, World Bank Institute**
>
> A symposium entitled Strengthening Governance for Infrastructure Service Delivery: The Role of Public Private Partnerships, held in Manila in March 2009, presented pragmatic governance learning materials to staff from participating training institutions. The symposium's ultimate goal was to help strengthen these institutions' learning programs to.better address the governance capacity-building requirements of the public sector in their respective countries. Its interactive format allowed participants from across the Asia-Pacific region to apply the principles of the Learning Spiral to assess the strategic design of the MP3IC learning materials, and determine the effectiveness of the symposium in engaging educators and academics from across the Asia Pacific region in the MP3IC design process.
>
> The Learning Spiral was introduced at the symposium's outset. Its framework helped focus the delegates' discussion on the challenges of government training and e-learning processes, and helped them consider the role of learning materials in this context. The framework has helped guide the design of learning delivery strategies for public sector officials with its emphasis on cutting-edge pedagogy and multimedia technology to transform research findings and practice into messages that developing-country public sector professionals can use in their day-to-day problem solving.
>
> *(Box continues on the following page.)*

---

4. The event had the title *MP3IC Knowledge Sharing Symposium—PPP's for Infrastructure in the Asia Pacific: Global Challenges and Constraints* and was held December 16–17, 2009.

> **Box 6 (*continued*)**
>
> The eight stages of the Learning Spiral provided a structured approach to develop the MP3IC global training and e-learning initiative, while also improving its strategic direction. Each stage provided a checklist of consideration points; these included the need to understand the learning requirements of the target audience. The eight stages also include reference to the need to identify effective learning access and delivery options, as well as the need to select content whose relevance is tested by target audiences. Finally, the stages include references to the steps needed to guarantee that knowledge transformation is achieved, and to make a reassessment to appropriately configure the next spin of the Learning Spiral.
>
> The Learning Spiral concept served as a constructive platform for exploring critical pedagogy challenges and evaluating and strengthening the strategic design of the MP3IC global learning program.
>
> Prior to the symposium, MP3IC had already begun to engage with the target audience through surveys, focus group discussions, and workshops held across the Asia-Pacific region. This allowed for pilot testing of the learning materials at different stages of development among diverse audience groups, including senior infrastructure policy makers, infrastructure program and project managers, and a broad range of technical practitioners. It also involved technical and pedagogy specialists in design and development, as well as an exhaustive quality review of all learning materials. The symposium was an important part of the consultation process, as it enabled in-depth discussion with potential partners on learning content and delivery, to explore areas of synergy and pragmatic business models for collaboration.
>
> Govindan G. Nair, Washington, DC, USA, March 27, 2010

10 Conclusions and Outlook

Today, there is still little known about the concrete mechanisms that enhance learning in governments. Many perceive the gaps between inputs and outcomes in a learning system as an inscrutable black box. The Learning Spiral is an attempt to illuminate the contents of that box with a theory-derived and practice-approved learning concept. Its systematic presentation in this volume with its linear chains of action and simultaneous iterative processes turned out to be an ambitious challenge. In this concluding reflection, the Learning Spiral is therefore summarized one more time to clarify its main characteristics. To further develop this concept it must continuously be evaluated and adapted to changes in practice and to new related research findings.

10.1 Conclusions

The Learning Spiral is a concept that is designed to organize events in which governmental learning is taking place. It is an instrument to enhance behavioral change in governments through prearranged learning events, such as conferences, e-learning, training, etc., in order to improve performance in democratic governance. As demonstrated in the case studies in chapters 5 through 9, the Learning Spiral template is applicable to a wide range of types of governmental learning events. The overall ratings of the Level One evaluations, as well as the testimonies by selected participants a few years after the events took place, prove the positive impact of these learning activities (see Boxes 1–6).

However, following the rationale of the presented results framework, more rigorous evaluation of the concept and its application is required for a comprehensible validation of its effectiveness and to derive evidence for its future development. It is also essential to remember that such learning events, as important as they are, do have their limits, considering the complex political reality in which governments operate. There are numerous mechanisms and processes that provoke resistance and barriers to governmental learning and that need special attention. And even if a learning event succeeds and does create the expected behavioral change, there will always be many more factors involved that do have an unpredictable and uncontrollable impact on the overall performance of a given government. Even more uncertainty remains regarding to what extent this change will finally result in a reduction of poverty and an increase in sustainable development, as the international community postulated in the MDGs.

Nevertheless, properly organized governmental learning events can make a difference in a government's improving its democratic governance system or at least some important aspects of it. This strong belief in the efficacy of the concept is not only based on its successful application in numerous events around the world, but also in its theory-based development, which reflects a wide range of scientific disciplines. The concept is derived from a multitude of theories related to the subject that were carefully reviewed in a qualitative content analysis about their contribution to developing the Learning Spiral. In these terms this book is a research endeavor in itself, where analytical and theoretical considerations were systematically examined and made operational in order to develop a heuristic concept that can be used to design effective governmental learning events.

The concept uses a unique eight-stage template, which structures a learning activity based on the specific consistency of the knowledge a government wants to learn as well as its particular political and institutional environment, which determines the selection of the learning actors. These carefully chosen participants represent different content and organizational perspectives and play a precisely defined role, which implies that they are both knowledge holders and knowledge seekers. Every participant is considered an active contributor who shares his or her experiences with his or her peers. In this kind of procedure, participants have unlimited access to the collective wealth of the shared knowledge.

The successful launch and completion of this process requires the oversight of a learning broker who is backed up by an institutional support system in the form of a learning agency; this ensures the iterative character of the Learning Spiral, as well as its long-term development. The practical application of the template itself needs to be adapted to every new learning situation and should bring together the knowledge content with the design of the learning process. Because there are always constraints that limit the full implementation of the eight stages, it is the learning broker's responsibility to decide where compromises can be made to ensure an optimal performance of the overall learning process.

This process is an integrated part of a broader learning system. Its purpose is to enhance the implementation of a diagnosed, selected, and disseminated set of normative knowledge in a particular governmental setting. In the course of this learning process, that knowledge is reviewed in a real-time procedure and complemented with the latest experiences of the learning actors. In this kind of action learning, new knowledge is continuously validated and updated and as a consequence becomes in a type of feedback loop (the Learning Spiral) the potential new state-of-the-art knowledge for other learning systems.

Furthermore, the application the Learning Spiral evokes a sense of social belonging among the learning actors and as leads to the creation of networks and communities of practice. In these networks the participants' experiences are continuously exchanged and transformed, which relaunches a potential next spin of the Learning Spiral. Such a continuous knowledge exchange between learning actors can ensure sustainable governmental learning.

10.2 Outlook

To face today's difficult challenges, governments must necessarily strive to improve themselves on an ongoing basis. Since the emergence of the modern state, governments developed into a complex architecture of different organizational bodies, composed of numerous policy actors and managing (polity) a growing number of principles (policy) and tasks, which are directed to match citizens' needs and expectations (politics). To successfully handle these challenges and to improve capacities in democratic governance, governments have to be ready to learn from their past and others' experiences, as well as to become open to sharing their experiences with each other.

The Learning Spiral is a concept that incorporates all these requirements. However, as the challenges of democratic governance in a globalized world change and expand, the concept itself has to adapt and develop accordingly. In this understanding, the Learning Spiral is a work in progress. As has been the case since its first application more than a decade ago, it is expected that new insights gained from evaluations of future events and new theories related to the subject will lead to adjustments and improvements of the concept. Practitioners and theoreticians alike are therefore invited to engage in this dialogue launched by *The Black Box of Governmental Learning*. If this is done systematically and consistently, it is expected that the collected experiences and reflections could lead to the development of a generic and broadly accepted *theory of governmental learning*.

As shown in the case study about a global multimedia learning initiative (see chapter 9), the role of new social media technologies will have a significant impact in the future shape and quality of learning in governments. It therefore will be critical to carefully review forthcoming innovations regarding their potential contributions to improving the Learning Spiral.

Despite the expected gains of these innovations, it will be always important that the learning events themselves do not end up overly designed. The process of governmental learning has to be as comprehensible and explicable as possible so the learning actors fully understand how and why a particular learning event is organized as it is and so they are in a position to judge if the event fits their particular needs and expectations. In this understanding a successful governmental learning event should be always driven by demand.

The Learning Spiral was applied and developed for democratic governmental systems or governments that want to transform their existing political systems into democratic ones. However, the question is raised to what extent the concept or at least some aspects of it may be applicable in other governmental systems, such as autocracies, monarchies, or different forms of tribal communities. A similar argument could be made about its applicability in nongovernmental settings like businesses or civil society organizations. These are legitimate questions, which should find further attention in future research.

Given that only a fraction of the resources invested in the creation of knowledge in democratic governance is used for the actual application of that knowledge, there is a strong sense of urgency today that all available means should be fully devoted to the organization and improvement of future governmental learning processes. There is a significant backlog and a real need to improve such targeted learning in governmental events. By the increased and widespread application of the Learning Spiral, not only will an important contribution to improving performance in governments be available, but also new practice relevant knowledge in democratic governance will be generated and new content-related networks created worldwide. This in turn will contribute to the further development of the Learning Spiral.

Bibliography

Abderhalden, U., and R. Blindenbacher. 2002. *Federalism in a Changing World—Learning from Each Other*. Conference Reader. Bern: Second International Conference on Federalism 2002.

ADB (Asian Development Bank). 2009. *Knowledge Solutions: Tools, Methods, Approaches to Drive Development Forward and Enhance Its Effort*. Manila: Asian Development Bank.

Alston, Lee J., Trainn Eggertsson, and Douglass C. North (eds.). 1996. *Empirical Studies in Institutional Change*. Cambridge: Cambridge University Press.

Andrews, Matthew. 2008a. "Creating Space for Effective Political Engagement in Development." HKS Faculty Research Working Paper Series RWP08-015. Boston: John F. Kennedy School of Governance.

———. 2008b. "Effective Political Engagement." In Sina Odugbemi and Thomas Jacobson, eds. *Governance Reform under Real World Conditions*. Washington DC: World Bank.

———. 2010. "Good Government Means Different Things in Different Countries." *Governance* 23 (1): 7–35.

———. Forthcoming. "The Limits of Externally Motivated Public Financial Management Reform." *Journal of Public Administration Research and Theory*.

Andrews, Matthew, Jesse McConnell, and Alison Wescott. 2010. "Development as Leadership-Led Change." HKS Faculty Research Working Paper Series RWP10-009. Boston: John F.Kennedy School of Governance.

Argyris, Chris. 1982. *Reasoning, Learning, and Action*. San Francisco: Jossey-Bass Publishers.

———. 1990. *Overcoming Organizational Defenses—Facilitating Organizational Learning*. Boston: Allyn and Bacon.

Argyris, Chris, and Donald Schoen. 1974. *Theory in Practice: Increasing Professional Effectiveness.* San Francisco: Jossey Bass.

———. 1978. *Organizational Learning: A Theory of Action Perspective.* Reading, MA: Addison Wesley.

———. 1996. *Organizational Learning II: Theory, Method and Practice.* Reading, MA: Addison Wesley.

Bandura, A. 1977. *Social Learning Theory.* Englewood Cliffs, NJ: Prentice Hall.

Bateson, G., D.D. Jackson, J. Haley, and J.H. Weakland. 1956. "Toward a Theory of Schizophrenia." *Behavioral Science.* 1: 251–264.

Batterbury, Simon P.J., and Jude L. Fernando. 2006. "Rescaling Governance and the Impacts of Political and Environmental Decentralization: An Introduction." *World Development* 34 (11): 1851–1863.

Baus, Thomas, Raoul Blindenbacher, and Ulrich Karpen (eds.). 2007. *Competition versus Cooperation: German Federalism in Need of Reform—A Comparative Perspective.* Baden-Baden: Nomos.

Bayne, Nicolas, and Robert D. Putnam. 2000. *Hanging in There: The G7 and G8 Summit in Maturity and Renewal.* Surrey, UK: Ashgate Publishing.

Beery, Jenny, Esther Eidinow, and Nancy Murphy, eds. 2009. *The Mont Fleur Scenarios: What Will South Africa Be Like in the Year 2002?* Emeryville CA: Global Business Network.

Bennett, C,J., and M. Howlett. 1992. "The Lessons of Learning: Reconciling Theories of Policy Learning and Policy Change." *Policy Sciences* 25: 275–294.

Bell, Daniel. 1976. *The Coming of Post-Industrial Society.* New York: Basic Books.

Blindenbacher, Raoul. 1997. *Organisationsstrukturen Sozialer Einrichtungen. Ein Strukturierungsprogramm zur Steigerung der Wirksamkeit Sozialer Einrichtungen.* Bern, Stuttgart, Wien: Verlag Paul Haupt.

———. 1999. "The Task Dilemma in Human Service Organizations and Its Impact on Efficacy. A Possible Solution Developed Out of the Theory of Society of Juergen Habermas." *European Journal of Social Work* 2 (2): 131–138.

Blindenbacher, Raoul, and Barbara Brook. 2005. "A Global Dialogue on Federalism." In *Dialogues on Constitutional Origins, Structure, and Change in Federal Countries*, R. Blindenbacher and Abigail Ostien, eds. Montreal: McGill-Queen's University Press.

Blindenbacher, Raoul, and Rupak Chattopadhyay. 2007. "History of the International Conference on Federalism." In *Unity in Diversity— Learning from Each Other*, Conference Reader. New Delhi: Fourth International Conference on Federalism 2007.

Blindenbacher, Raoul, and A. Koller (eds.). 2003. *Federalism in a Changing World: Learning from Each Other*. Montreal: McGill-Queen's University Press.

Blindenbacher, Raoul, and Bidjan Nashat. Forthcoming. "The Learning Spiral—A Concept to Share Knowledge for Development." In *Sharing Knowledge for Development: In Search of Best Practice*. Seoul: Korean Development Institute.

Blindenbacher, Raoul, and Chandra Pasma. 2007. *Dialoges on Foreign Relations in Federal Countries*. Montreal: McGill-Queen's University Press.

Blindenbacher, Raoul, and Cheryl Saunders. 2005. "A Global Dialogue on Federalism." In *Constitutional Origins, Structure, and Change in Federal Countries*, J. Kincaid and A.G. Tarr, eds. Montreal: McGill-Queen's University Press.

Blindenbacher, Raoul, and Ronald, L. Watts. 2003. "Federalism in a Changing World: A Conceptual Framework for the Conference." In *Federalism in a Changing World: Learning from Each Other*, R. Blindenbacher and A. Koller, eds. Montreal: McGill-Queen's University Press.

Blindenbacher, Raoul, Peter Habluetzel, and Bruno Letsch, eds. 2000. *Vom Service Public zum Service au Public. Regierung und Verwaltung auf dem Weg in die Zukunft*. Zuerich: Verlag Neue Zuercher Zeitung.

Blindenbacher, Raoul, Jakob Huber, and Andrea Iff. 2001. "Im Dialog zu einem neuen Fuehrungsverstaendnis." In: *Fuehren im Wandel. Regierung und Verwaltung an der Schwelle zur Wissensgesellschaft*. Schriftenreihe des Eidgenoessischen Personalamtes, Volume 14. Bern: 2001.

Blunt, Peter. 1995. "Cultural Relativism, 'Good' Governance and Sustainable Human Development." *Public Administration and Development* 15: 1–9.

Boas, Franz.1948. *Race, Language and Culture*. New York: Macmillan.

Boston, Jonathan, Stephen Levine, Elisabeth Mcleay, and Nigel S. Roberts (eds.). 1996. *New Zealand under MMP. A New Politics.* Auckland: Auckland University Press.

Campbell, Donald T., and Donald Fiske. 1959. "Convergent and Discriminant Validation by the Multitrait-Multimethod Matrix." *Psychological Bulletin* Volume: 56, 2: 81-105.

Chapman, Jake. 2002. *System Failure: Why Governments Must Learn to Think Differently*. London: DEMOS.

Chattopadhyay, Rupak, John Kincaid, and Ronald L. Watts, eds. 2008. *Unity in Diversity: Learning from Each Other*. New Delhi: Viva Books.

Cohen, Joshua, and Joel Rogers. 1992. "Secondary Associations and Democratic Governance." *Politics and Society* 20 (4): 393–472.

Connor, R., and S. Dovers. 2004. *Institutional Change for Sustainable Development*. Cheltenham: Edward Elgar.

Cowan, Robin, P. David, and D. Foray. 2000. "The Explicit Economics of Knowledge Codification and Tacitness." *Industrial and Corporate Change* 9: 211–253.

Cutting, Bruce, and Alexander Kouzmin. 1999. "From Chaos to Patterns of Understanding: Reflections on the Dynamics of Effective Government Decision Making." *Public Administration* 77 (3).

DAC (Development Assistance Committee). 2005. *The Paris Declaration and AAA*. Paris: http://www.oecd.org/document/18/0,3343,en_2649_3236398_35401554_1_1_1_1,00.html.

———. 2006. *The Challenge of Capacity Development: Working Towards Good Practice*. Paris: DAC Network on Governance Capacity Paper (GOVNET).

Davenport, Thomas H., Laurence Prusak, and Bruce Strong. 2008. "Putting Ideas to Work: Knowledge Management Can Make a Difference—But It Needs to Be More Pragmatic." *MIT Sloan Management Review.* http://sloanreview.mit.edu/.

Deutsch, Karl W. 1963. *The Nerves of Government: Models of Political Communication and Control.* New York: Free Press.

Dewey, J.1933. *How We Think: A Restatement of the Relation of Reflective Thinking to the Educative Process.* Boston; New York: D. C. Heath and Company.

Digital 4Sight. 2002. *Using Technology to Scale Up the World Bank's Impact.* Toronto: Digital 4Sight.

Dolowitz, David, and David Marsh. 2000. "Learning from Abroad: The Role of Policy Transfer in Contemporary Policy Making." *Governance: An International Journal of Policy and Administration* 13 (1): 9.

Doornbos, Martin. 2003. "'Good Governance': The Metamorphosis of a Policy Metaphor." *Journal of International Affairs* 57 (1): 3–17.

———. 2007. "Good Governance: The Metamorphosis of a Policy Metaphor." In *Public Governance: Democratic Governance,* Mark Bevir, ed. Thousand Oaks, CA: Sage Publications.

Dreze, Jean, and Amartya Sen. 1989. *Hunger and Public Action.* Oxford: Oxford University Press.

Dunleavy, Patrick. 1991. *Democracy, Bureaucracy and Public Choice.* London: Harvester Wheatsheaf.

Easton, David. 1965a. *A Framework for Political Analysis.* Englewood Cliffs, NJ: Prentice-Hall.

———. 1965b. *A Systems Analysis of Political Life.* New York: Wiley.

Edwards, Mark. 2000: http://www.integralworld.net/edwards2.html.

Eggerston, T. 1990. *Economic Behavior and Institutions.* New York: Cambridge University Press.

Encyclopedia Britannica. 2008 "The Online Encyclopedia." http://www.britannica.com/eb/article-9106262/government.

Etheredge, Lloyd S. 1981. "Government Learning: An Overview." In *Handbook of Political Behavior,* Samuel L. Long, ed. New York: Plenum Press.

Finer, S.E. 1997. *History of Government from the Earliest Times.* London: Oxford University Press.

Finkle, J.L., and R.W. Gable. 1971. *Political Development and Social Change.* New York: Wiley.

Fischer, Frank, and John Forester, John, eds. 1993. *The Argumentative Turn in Policy Analysis and Planning.* Durham, NC: Duke University Press.

Fischer, Frank, Gerald J. Miller, and Mara S. Sidney, eds. 2007. *Handbook of Public Policy Analysis. Theory, Politics, and Methods.* Boca Raton, FL: CRC Press.

Fleck, J. 1997. "Contingent Knowledge and Technology Development." *Technology Analysis and Strategic Management* 9: 383–397.

Gastil, John. 2009. "A Comprehensive Approach to Evaluating Deliberative Public Engagement." In *Engaging with Impact: Targets and Indicators for Successful Community Engagement by Ontario's Local Health Integration Networks: A Citizens' Report from Kingston, Richmond Hill and Thunder Bay,* MASS LBP. http://www.masslbp.com/media/engagingreport.pdf.

General Information Brochure. 2002. *International Conference on Federalism 2002.* August 27–30, St. Gallen, Switzerland.

Geerkens, Frank, ed. 2005. *Federalism: Turning Diversity into Harmony—Sharing Best Practices.* Brussels: Federal Public Service Foreign Affairs, Foreign Trade and Development Cooperation.

Global Development Learning Network. http://www.gdln.org/services/design.

Goldsmith, Arthur. 2004. "How Good Does Governance Need to Be? Historical Perspectives on Economic Development." Paper presented at the annual meeting of the American Political Science Association, Chicago.

Goldstein, Irwin L., and J. Kevin Ford. 2002. *Training in Organizations: Needs Assessment, Development and Evaluation.* Belmont: Wadsworth.

Graham, C. R. 2005. "Blended Learning Systems: Definition, Current Trends, and Future Directions." In *Handbook of Blended Learning: Global Perspectives,* Local Designs, C.J. Bonk and C.R. Graham, eds., 3–21. San Francisco: Pfeiffer.

Graham, John, Bruce Amos, and Tim Plumptre. 2003. *Principles of Good Governance in the 21st Century.* Policy Brief No. 15. Institute in Governance, Ottawa, http://www.iog.ca/publications/policybrief15.pdf.

Grin, John, and Anne Loeber. 2007. "Theories of Policy Learning: Agency, Structure and Change." In *Handbook of Public Policy Analysis. Theory, Politics, and Methods,* Frank Fischer, Gerald J. Miller, and Mara S. Sidney, eds., 201–219. CRC Press–Taylor & Francis Group.

Grindle, Merilee S. 2004. "Good Enough Governance: Poverty Reduction and Reform in Developing Countries." *Governance: An International Journal of Policy, Administration, and Institutions* 17 (4): 525–548.

Group of G-6. Wikipedia: http://en.wikipedia.org/wiki/G8.

Ha-Joon, Chang. 2000. *Institutional Development in Developing Countries in a Historical Perspective: Lessons from Developed Countries in Earlier Times.* Cambridge: University of Cambridge.

Habermas, Juergen. 1987a. *The Theory of Communicative Action.* Boston: Beacon Press.

———. 1987b. *Liveworld and System: A Critique of Functionalist Reason.* Boston: Beacon Press.

Habluetzel, T., T. Haldemann, K. Schedler, and K. Schwaar eds. 1995. *Umbruch in Politik und Verwaltung. Ansichten und Erfahrungen zum New Public Management in der Schweiz.* Bern, Stuttgart und Wien: Paul Haupt Verlag.

Hartley, James. 1998. *Learning and Studying: A Research Perspective.* London: Routledge.

Herbst, J.I. 2000. *States and Power in Africa: Comparative Lessons in Authority and Control.* Princeton, NJ: Princeton University Press.

Herzberg, Benjamin; and Andrew Wright. 2006. *The PPD Handbook: A Toolkit for Business Environment Reformers.* London and Washington, DC: DFID, IFC, World Bank, OECD http://www.publicprivatedialogue.org/papers/PPD%20handbook.pdf.

Hildreth, Paul M., and Chris Kimble. 2002. "The Duality of Knowledge." *Information Research* 8 (1).

Hoebink, Paul. 2006. "European Donors and 'Good Governance': Condition or Goal?" *European Journal of Development Research* 18 (1): 131–161.

Hubbard, Ruth. 1999. "Criteria of Good Governance." *Optimum, Journal of Public Management* 30 (2).

IEG (Independent Evaluation Group). 2003. *Sharing Knowledge. Innovations and Remaining Challenges.* Washington, DC: World Bank.

———. 2005. *Capacity Building in Africa.* Washington, DC: World Bank.

———. 2007a. *Annual Review of Development Effectiveness 2006. Getting Results.* Washington, DC: World Bank.

———. 2007b. *Decentralization in Client Countries: An Evaluation of World Bank Support, 1997–2007.* Washington, DC: World Bank.

———. 2008a. *Using Training to Build Capacity for Development. An Evaluation of the World Bank's Project-Based and WBI Training.* Washington, DC: World Bank.

———. 2008b. *Public Sector Reform: What Works and Why?* Washington, DC: World Bank.

———. 2008c. *Country Financial Accountability Assessments and Country Procurement Assessment Reports: How Effective Are World Bank Fiduciary Diagnostics?* Washington, DC: World Bank.

———. 2008d. *Using Knowledge to Improve Development Effectiveness. An Evaluation of World Bank Economic and Sector Work and Technical Assistance, 2000–2006.* Washington, DC: World Bank.

———. 2008e. *Workshop Findings: Lessons of a Decade of Public Sector Reform: Voices of African Client Stakeholders.* Washington, DC: World Bank. http://siteresources.worldbank.org/EXTOED/Resources/addis_findings_opt1.pdf.

Iqbal, Kazi, and Anwar Shah. 2008. "How Do Worldwide Governance Indicators Measure Up?" Unpublished paper, World Bank, Washington, DC.

Isaacs, B. 1999. *The Dialogue and the Art of thinking Together.* New York: Doubleday.

Isaacs, William N. 1998. *Dialogue and the Art of Thinking Together: A Pioneering Approach to Communicating in Business and in Life.* New York: Doubleday.

Kaufmann, Daniel, Aart Kraay, and Massimo Mastruzzi. 2009. *The World Governance Indicators, 1996–2008.* Washington, DC: World Bank. http://www.worldbank.org/wbi/governance.

Kemp, Rene, and Rifka Weehuizen. 2005. "Policy Learning, What Does It Mean and How Can We Study It?" Report No. D15. Oslo: NIFU STEP.

Kerber, Wolfgang, and Martina Eckardt. 2005. "Policy Learning in Europe: The 'Open Method of Coordination' and Laboratory Federalism." Thuenen-Series of Applied Economic Theory. Working Paper No. 48.

King, Kenneth, and Simon McGrath. 2002. "Knowledge Sharing in Development Agencies: Lessons from Four Cases." Background Paper, Independent Evaluation Group, Washington, DC.

Kirkpatirck, Donald.L. 1998. *Evaluating Training Programs: The Four Levels.* San Francisco: Berrett-Koehler Publishers.

Koeberle, Stefan, Harold Bedoya, Peter Silarsky, and Gero Verheyen, eds. 2005: *Conditionality Revisited Concepts, Experiences, and Lessons.* Washington, DC: World Bank.

Koller, Arnold. 2003. "Schlussbericht der Internationalen Foederalismuskonferenz 2002." Bern: Unpublished Document.

Kooiman, J., and Van Vliet, M. 1993. "Governance and Public Management." In *Managing Public Organizations,* K. Eliassen and J. Kooiman, eds. London: Sage.

Krippendorff, K. 1969. "Models of Messages: Three Prototypes." In *The Analysis of Communication Content,* G. Gerbner, O.R. Holsti, K. Krippendorff, G.J. Paisly, and P.J. Stone, eds. New York: Wiley.

Krohwinkel-Karlsson, Anna. 2007. *Knowledge and Learning in Aid Organizations.* SADEV Report 2007:3, Swedish Agency for Development Evaluation, http://www.sadev.se/Uploads/Files/151.pdf.

Kusek, J., and R. Rist. 2004. *Ten Steps to a Results-Based Monitoring and Evaluation System: A Handbook for Development Practitioners.* Washington, DC: World Bank.

Laporte, Bruno. 2004. "The Evolution of the Knowledge Bank." *World Bank* 7 (6).

Lave, J., and E. Wenger. 1991. *Situated Learning. Legitimate Peripheral Participation.* Cambridge: University of Cambridge Press.

Leeuw, Frans, and Richard C Sonnichsen. 1994. "Introduction: Evaluations and Organizational Learning: International Perspectives." In *Can Governments Learn? Comparative Perspectives on Evaluation and Organizational Learning*, Frans Leeuw, Ray C. Rist, and Richard C. Sonnichsen, eds., 1–16. New Brunswick and London: Transaction Publishers.

Leeuw, Frans, Ray C. Rist, and Richard C. Sonnichsen. 1994. *Can Governments Learn? Comparative Perspectives on Evaluation and Organizational Learning.* New Brunswick and London: Transaction Publishers.

Leonard, D., and S. Sensiper. 1998. "The Role of Tacit Knowledge in Group Innovation." *California Management Review* 40 (3): 112–132.

Lewin, K. 1935. *A Dynamic Theory of Personality.* New York: McGraw-Hill.

Lockheed, Marlaine E. 2009. "Evaluating Development Learning: The World Bank Experience." *Evaluation* 15: 113–126.

Machiavelli, Niccolo. 1532. *"The Prince."* 2008 version: Edison, NJ: Chartwell Books, Inc.

Mackay, Keith. 1998. *The 1997 Conference of the Mediterranean Development Forum: An Evaluation of a Pilot Initiative.* EDI Evaluation Studies. Washington, DC: World Bank.

March, James G., and Johan P. Olsen. 1995. *Democratic Governance.* New York: The Free Press.

Maslow. A. 1970. *Motivation and Personality.* New York: Harper and Row.

May, P.J. 1992. "Policy Learning and Policy Failure." *Journal of Public Policy* 12: 331–354.

Mead. G.H. 1934. *Mind, Self and Society.* Chicago: University of Chicago Press.

Meekison, J. Peter. 2007. *A Global Dialogue on Federalism. Program Evaluation*. Prepared for The Forum of Federations and the International Association of Centers for Federal Studies. Ottawa.

Michalewicz, Zbigniew, and David B. Fogel. 2000. *How to Solve It: Modern Heuristics*. New York: Springer-Verlag.

Michelmann, Hans. 2009. *Foreign Relations in Federal Countries*. Montreal: McGill-Queen's University Press.

Michels, Roberto. 1911. *Political Parties: A Sociological Study of the Oligarchic Tendencies of Modern Democracy*. Electronic Text Center, University of Virginia Library: http://etext.lib.virginia.edu/toc/mod-eng/public/MicPoli.html.

Morra Imas, Linda G., and Ray Rist. 2009. *The Road to Results: Designing and Conducting Effective Development Evaluations*. Washington, DC: World Bank.

Nashat, Bidjan. 2008. *Learning from Evaluation at the UN Office on Drugs and Crime: A Case Study Analysis of the Evaluation Process*. Saarbruecken: VDM Publishing.

Nevis, E. C., A.J. DiBella, and J.M. Gould. 1995. "Understanding Organizations as Learning Systems." *Sloan Management Review* 36 (2): 75–85.

Nonaka, I. 1991. "The Knowledge Creating Company." *Harvard Business Review* 69 (12): 96–104.

Nonaka, Ikujiro, and Noboru Konno. 1998. "The Concept of 'Ba': Building a Foundation for Knowledge Creation. *California Management Review* 40 (3): 40–54.

OECD (Organisation for Economic Co-operation and Development). 2003-2004. *Assessment Methodology for Public Procurements Systems*. Paris: OECD. http://www.oedc.org/dac.

Openspace-Online: http://www.change-management-blog.com/2007/07/worldwide-openspace-online-real-time.html.

Osterloh, M., and S. Wübker. 2000. *Wettbewerbsfaehiger durch Prozess und Wissensmanagement*. Wiesbaden: Gaebler.

Otoo, Samuel, Natalia Agapitova, and Joy Behrens. 2009. *The Capacity Development Results Framework—A Strategic And Results Oriented*

Approach to Learning for Capacity Development. Washington, DC: World Bank Institute. http://go.worldbank.org/D4NG0SXH60.

Owen, Harrison. 1997. *Open Space Technology: A User's Guide.* San Francisco: Berrett-Koehler.

Pavlov, Ivan Petrovich. 1927. *Conditioned Reflexes.* London: Oxford University Press

Parsons, Talcott. 1951. *The Social System.* Glencoe, IL: The Free Press.

Perrin, Burt, and Keith Mackay. 1999. *What Makes for Successful Conferences? Lessons Learned from an Evaluation of Six Conferences Sponsored by the World Bank Institute.* WBI Evaluation Studies. Number ES99-34 World Bank Institute, Washington, DC. http://go.worldbank.org/IZ3Y6FN6M0.

Peters, Guy B. 1998. *Comparative Politics. Theory and Methods.* New York: New York University Press.

Piaget, Jean. 1926. *The Child's Conception of the World.* London: Routledge and Kegan Paul.

Pleasant Breeden, James. 1972. *Policy, Polity and Politics: The Primary School Board of Boston: 1818–1855.* Boston: Harvard Graduate School of Education.

Polanyi, Michael. 1967. *The Tacit Dimension.* London: Routledge.

Popper, Karl. 1959. *The Logic of Scientific Discovery.* London: Hutchison.

Punyaratabandhy, Suchitra. 2004. "Commitment to Good Governance, Development, and Poverty Reduction: Methodological Issues in the Evaluation of Progress at National and Local Levels." Paper Prepared for the Sixth Session of the Committee on Development Policy. National Institute of Development Administration. Bangkok, Thailand.

Ramsden, Paul. 1992. *Learning to Teach in Higher Education.* London: Routledge.

Raskin, Paul, Tariq Banuri, Gilberto Gallopin, Pablo Gutman, Al Mammond, Robert Kates, and Rob Swart. 2002. *Great Transition.* "The Promise and Lure of the Times Ahead." A report of the Global Scenario Group. Stockholm Environment Institute and the Boston Tellus Institute, Stockholm and Boston. http://www.gtinitiative.org/documents/great_transitions.pdf.

Rist, Ray C. 1994. "The Preconditions for Learning: Lessons from the Public Sector." In *Can Governments Learn? Comparative Perspectives on Evaluation and Organizational Learning*, Frans Leeuw, Ray C. Rist, and Richard C. Sonnichsen, eds., 189–206. New Brunswick and London: Transaction Publishers.

Rodrik, Dani, ed. 2003. *Search of Prosperity: Analytic Narratives on Economic Growth*. Princeton: Princeton University Press.

Rogers, A. 2003. *What Is the Difference? A New Critique of Adult Learning and Teaching*. Leicester: NIACE.

Rogers, C., and H.J. Freiberg. 1993. *Freedom to Learn*. New York: Merrill.

Rose, Richard. 1991. "What Is Lesson Drawing?" *Journal of Public Policy* 11 (1): 3–30.

———. 1993. *Lessons-Drawing in Public Policy. A Guide to Learning across Time and Space*. Chatham, NJ: Chatham House Publishers.

———. 2004. *Learning from Comparative Public Policy. A Practical Guide*. London and New York: Routledge.

Rotberg, Robert, I. 2004/05. "Strengthening Governance: Ranking Countries Would Help." *The Washington Quarterly* 28 (1): 71–81.

Sabatier, Paul A. 1987. "Knowledge, Policy-Oriented Learning, and Policy Change. An Advocacy Coalition Framework." *Knowledge* 8: 649–692.

Sabatier, Paul A., and Hank C. Jenkins-Smith (eds). 1993. *Policy Change and Learning: An Advocacy Coalition Approach*. Colorado: Westview Press.

Santiso, Carlos. 2001. "International Co-Operation for democracy and Good Governance: Moving Towards a Second Generation?" *European Journal of Development Research* 13 (1): 154–180.

Schaffer, Robert H., and Ronald N. Ashkenas. 2005. *Rapid Results! How 100-Day Projects Build the Capacity for Large-Scale Change*. San Francisco: Jossey-Bass.

Schein, Edgar H., ed. 2004. *Organizational Culture and Leadership*. San Francisco: Jossey-Bass.

———. 1998. *Process Consultation Revisited: Building the Helping Relationship*. New Jersey: Prentice-Hall.

Schoemaker, Paul J.H. 1995. "Scenario Planning: A Tool for Strategic Thinking." *Sloan Management Review* (Winter): 25–40.

Schoen, Donald, and Martin Rein. 1994. *Frame Reflection: Toward the Resolution of Intractable Policy Controversies*. New York: Basic Books.

Schriftenreihe des Eidgenoessischen Personalamtes. 1998-2001. Band 10–14. Bern: EDMZ.

Senge, Peter M. 1998. *The Fifth Discipline: The Art & Practice of the Learning Organization*. Sydney: Random House Australia.

SIDA (Swedish International Development Co-operation Agency). 2003. *Country Strategy Development: Guide for Country Analysis from a Democratic Governance and Human Rights Perspective*. http://www.humanrights.se/upload/files/2/R%E4ttighetsperspektivet/Guide%20for%20Country%20Analysis-%20Sida.pdf.

Skinner, B.F. 1973. *Beyond Freedom and Dignity*. London: Penguin.

Skinner, Quentin. 1989. "The State." In *Political Innovation and Conceptual Change*, T. Ball, J. Farr, and R.L. Hanson, eds. Cambridge: Cambridge University Press.

Simon, F.B. 1997. *Die Kunst, nicht zu lernen. Und andere Paradoxien in Psychotherapie, Management, Politik*. Heidelberg: Carl Auer Verlag.

Stoker, Gerry. 2000. *Governance as Theory: Five Propositions*. Oxford: Blackwell Publishers.

Sugrue, B., and K. Kim. 2004. *State of the Industry: ASTD's Annual Review of Trends in Workplace Learning and Performance*. Alexandria, VA: ASTD.

Tennant, M. 1997. *Psychology and Adult Learning*. London: Routledge.

Thatcher, Margaret. 2009. Archive of the Margaret Thatcher Foundation. http://www.margaretthatcher.org/archive/default.asp.

Tuchman, Barbara W. 1985. *The March of Folly: From Troy to Vietnam*. New York: Random House.

UN (United Nations). 2000a. New York: http://www.un.org/millenniumgoals/index.shtml.

———. 2000b. *United Nations End Poverty 2015 Program. Make It Happen*. United Nations, New York. http://www.un.org/millenniumgoals/index.shtml.

UNDP (United Nations Development Program). 1994. "Governance, Public Sector Management and Sustainable Human Development." UNDP Strategy Paper, New York.

Watson, John B. 1913. "Psychology as the Behaviorist Views It." *Psychological Review* 20: 158.

Watts, Ronald L. 2008. *Comparing Federal Systems*, 3rd ed. Montreal: McGill-Queen's University Press.

WBI (World Bank Institute). 2009. Washington, DC. http://web.worldbank.org/WBSITE/EXTERNAL/WBI/0,,pagePK:208996~theSitePK:213799,00.html.

Weber, Max. 1921. *Wirtschaft und Gesellschaft*. Tuebingen: J.C.B. Mohr (Paul Siebeck).

Weick, Karl E. 1995. *Der Prozess des Organisierens*. Frankfurt: Suhrkamp Verlag.

Wenger, Etienne. 1998. *Communities of Practice: Learning, Meaning, and Identity*. Cambridge: Cambridge University Press.

———. 2006: *Communities of Practice. A Brief Introduction*. http://www.ewenger.com/theory/index.htm.

———. 2008. *Communities of Practice at the World Bank*. Washington, DC: World Bank.

Whitney, Diana, and Amanda Trosten-Bloom. 2003. *Power of Appreciative Inquiry: A Practical Guide to Positive Change*. San Francisco: Berret-Koehler.

Williamson, John. 1989. "What Washington Means by Policy Reform." In *Latin American Readjustment: How Much Has Happened*, John Williamson ed. Washington, DC: Institute for International Economics.

Willke, H. 1993. *Systemtheorie Entwickelter Gesellschaften*. Weinheim/Muenchen: UTB.

———. 1997. *Supervision des Staates*. Frankfurt: Suhrkamp.

Wolfensohn, James. 1996. "People and Development." Annual Meetings Address, World Bank, Washington, DC.

Wood, Bernard, Kabell Dorte, Muwanga Nansozi, and Sagasti Francisco. 2008. *Evaluation of the Implementation of the Paris Declaration*.

Phase One. Synthesis Report. Koege, Denmark: Ministry of Foreign Affairs of Denmark.

World Bank. 1996–2008. *World Governance Indicators. Governance Matters.* Washington, DC: World Bank. http://info.worldbank.org/governance/wgi/sc_country.asp.

———. 1997. *World Development Report: The State in a Changing World.* New York and Washington, DC: Oxford University Press and World Bank.

———. 1998. World Development Report. 1998–1999. *Knowledge for Development.* New York and Washington, DC: Oxford University Press and World Bank.

———. 2005. *Review of World Bank Conditionality.* Washington, DC. http://web.worldbank.org/WBSITE/EXTERNAL/PROJECTS/0,,contentMDK:20292723~pagePK:41367~piPK:51533~theSitePK:40941,00.html.

———. 2007. *Global Monitoring Report. Millennium Development Goals. Confronting the Challenges of Gender Equality and Fragile States.* Washington, DC: World Bank.

———. 2008. *Poverty Data. A Supplement to World Development Indicators 2008.* Washington, DC. http://siteresources.worldbank.org/DATASTATISTICS/Resources/WDI08supplement1216.pdf.

———. 2009a. *World Development Report. 1997–2009. Reshaping Economic Geography.* New York: Oxford University Press.

———. 2009b. World Development Indicators. Washington, DC. http://web.worldbank.org/WBSITE/EXTERNAL/DATASTATISTICS/0,,contentMDK:21725423~pagePK:64133150~piPK:64133175~theSitePK:239419,00.html.

———. 2009c. Open Governance Initiative. Washington, DC. http://blogs.worldbank.org/publicsphere/category/tags/open-government-initiative.

World Social Forum. 2002. http://www.portoalegre2002.org/.

List of Boxes, Figures, Tables, and Photographs

Boxes

Box 1: Reflections from Deputy Chief Financial Officer and Chief Economist of the Washington, DC, Government

Box 2: Reflections on the Conference Process from the Former Premier of Ontario and Current Member of the Parliament of Canada

Box 3: Reflections from the Former President of Switzerland

Box 4: Reflections from the Chief Justice of the Federal Supreme Court and President of the Higher Judicial Council of Iraq

Box 5: Reflections from the Director of Planning and Programming Directorate, Ministry of Capacity Building of the Government of Ethiopia

Box 6: Reflections from the Lead Economist, Public-Private Partnerships, World Bank Institute

Figures

Figure 1: Democratic Government and Governance Conceptualized as a System

Figure 2: The Knowledge Creation Cycle

Figure 3: Knowledge Creation in Democratic Governance

Figure 4: Governmental Learning System

Figure 5: Analytical and Theoretical Concepts that Feed into the Learning Process

Figure 6: Selected Knowledge Frame

Figure 7: Perspectives Regarding the Knowledge Frame

Figure 8: Safeguarding the Knowledge Frame

Figure 9: Self-Positioning in Regard to the Knowledge Frame

Figure 10: Group Positioning in Regard to the Knowledge Frame

Figure 11: Reframing the Knowledge Frame

Figure 12: Deduction of the Knowledge Frame into Context

Figure 13: Distribution of the Revised Knowledge Frame

Figure 14: Sequences of the Learning Spiral Template

Figure 15: A Results Framework of the Learning System

Figure 16: Work Session Set Up

Figure 17: Dialogue Table Set Up 1

Figure 18: Dialogue Table Set Up 2

Figure 19: Dialogue Table Set Up 3

Tables

Table 1: Historic Approaches to Learning in Democratic Governments

Table 2: Knowledge Fabric

Table 3: Knowledge Fabric in Democratic Governance

Table 4: Individual Learning Theories

Table 5: Comparison of Different Levels of Organization

List of Boxes, Figures, Tables, and Photographs | **181**

Photographs

Photo 1: Work Session Roundtable

Photo 2: Dialogue Table Phase 1

Photo 3: Dialogue Table Phase 2

Photo 4: Dialogue Table Phase 3

Photo 5: Interactive Plenary Session

Photos 6–13: Global Dialogue Program Country Roundtables (Chicago, USA; Vienna, Austria; Brussels, Belgium; Berlin, German; New Delhi, India; Zürich, Switzerland; Brasilia, Brazil; Moscow, Russia)

Photos 14 and 15: Global Dialogue Program International Roundtable

Photo 16: Content Triangulation

Photos 17 and 18: Field Trips to Federal and Cantonal Courts

Photos 19 and 20: Reflection Sessions

Photo 21: Seating Order in Plenary Session

Photo 22: Plenary Session Moderation

Photo 23: Plenary Session

Photo 24: Breakout Group

Photo 25: Action Planning

All photographs ©Raoul Blindenbacher.

Author Biographies

Raoul Blindenbacher is an adviser to the World Bank's Independent Evaluation Group and the World Bank Institute on a secondment from the Swiss Ministry of Foreign Affairs since 2007. Prior to this assignment, he was the Vice President and Director Global Programs at the Forum of Federations. He is the author and editor of numerous publications in the field of institutional and intergovernmental learning and a lecturer at universities and international organizations worldwide. He earned a doctorate in education, organizational sociology, and political science from the University of Zurich.

Bidjan Nashat has been working at the Independent Evaluation Group's Communication, Learning and Strategy department as a consultant since 2008. Previously, he was an adviser to the Heinrich Boell Foundation on a multiyear transatlantic round table series on Middle Eastern security. He has done field research and published on learning from evaluation at the United Nations Office on Drugs and Crime. He studied Public Policy and International Relations at the Hertie School of Governance, and at Georgetown, Yale, and Tuebingen Universities and holds a Master of Public Policy and a Magister Artium.